designing
for interaction

SECOND EDITION

Creating Innovative

Applications and Devices

Dan Saffer

New

Designing for Interaction, Second Edition:
Creating Innovative Applications and Devices
Dan Saffer

New Riders
1249 Eighth Street
Berkeley, CA 94710
620/524-2178
510/524-2221 (fax)

Find us on the Web at: www.newriders.com
To report errors, please send a note to errata@peachpit.com

New Riders is an imprint of Peachpit, a division of Pearson Education

Project Editor: Michael J. Nolan
Development Editor: Box Twelve Communications, Inc.
Production Editor: Becky Winter
Copyeditor: Rose Weisburd
Proofreader: Darren Meiss
Indexer: James Minkin
Cover designer: Aren Howell
Interior designer: Andrei Pasternak with Maureen Forys

ISBN 13: 978-0-321-64339-1
ISBN 10:   0-321-64339-9
5 16
Printed and bound in the United States of America

Dedication

For Rachael, who puts up with me

Acknowledgements

The shadow of the two years I spent steeping in design at Carnegie Mellon University looms large over this book. When I wrote the first edition, I found myself constantly referring to my notes from that time and hearing the echoes of my professors' words, including those of Dan Boyarski, Kristen Hughes, Karen Moyer, John Zimmerman, and Jodi Forlizzi. I want to particularly note the influence of Dick Buchanan, who immeasurably broadened my understanding of this discipline, and my friend and advisor Shelley Evenson, who taught me at least half of what I know about interaction design. Without her knowledge and experience, poorly filtered through me, this book would be shallow indeed.

In the second edition, the influence of my professional colleagues at Adaptive Path and now Kicker Studio can be felt. Particular kudos to Adaptive Pathers Brandon Schauer, Peter Merholz, and especially Henning Fischer, who helped lead me, sometimes kicking and screaming, into the world of design strategy. This book is much improved for its inclusion. My Kicker Studio partners Jennifer Bove and Tom Maiorana have been generous with their editing and design help, not to mention encouragement.

My interviewees were generous with their time and expertise and I'd like to especially thank them. Your presence in my book honors me.

I'm also grateful to companies who lent their case studies and beautiful product images to the book, illustrating my points better than I could have with words alone.

The staff at Peachpit/New Riders has been a tremendous help in making this book what it is, in this edition and the last. My editors Michael Nolan, Becky Winter, and Jeff Riley have polished my rough edges (and there were many) into the fine tome you have in your hands (or on your screen). Another special thanks goes to my friend and technical editor Bill DeRouchey, whose insights burnished this book.

Other friends who have lent their support and help with both this edition and the last: Phi-Hong Ha, Jesse James Garrett, Andrew Crow, Jannine Takahashi-Crow, Kristina Halvorson, Marc Rettig, Adam Greenfield, Ryan Freitas, Rae Brune, Jennifer Fraser, Lane Becker, Brian Oberkirch, Chad Thorton, Rob Adams, Kenneth Berger, Willow Stelzer, Kim Lenox, Todd Wilkens, Uday Gajendar, Chiara Fox, Dave Malouf, Kim Goodwin,

Nancy Broden, Alan Cooper, Dana Smith, Rachel Hinman, Erika Hall, Rachel Glaves, Samantha Soma, Sarah Nelson, Jared Spool, Jody Medich, Mike Scully, Laura Kirkwood-Datta, Liz Danzico, Kevin Daly, Shinohara Toshikazu, Zach Hettinger, my in-laws Mary and Barry King, and my sister, Meagan Duffy.

Thanks to my parents, who bought me my first computer (a Timex Sinclair 1000) and a 300 baud modem and who paid the ensuing long-distance phone bills.

My daughter Fiona, a budding interaction designer herself, had to endure my writing when I could have been playing Wii with her. More time for Mario now.

Lastly, and most importantly, without the support of my wife, Rachael King, the creation of this book would have been impossible. All writers need time and space, and those are always her gifts to me. This book is as much a product of her generosity as it is of my words.

Contents

About the Author

Although he wouldn't hear the term "interaction design" for another decade and a half, Dan Saffer did his first interaction design work as a teenager in the mid-1980s when he designed and ran a dial-up game on his Apple IIe, a 2600-baud modem, two floppy disk drives, and a phone line. And yes, it was in his parents' basement.

He's worked formally in interactive media and product design since 1995 as a webmaster, information architect, copywriter, developer, producer, creative lead, creative director, and, of course, interaction designer. Currently, he's one of the founders and principals of Kicker Studio, a product design consultancy in San Francisco.

Dan has designed a wide range of products, from Web sites to interactive TV services, from mobile and medical devices, to touchscreens, gestural interfaces, and robots. His clients have included Fortune 100 companies, government agencies, and startups.

He holds a Masters in Design, Interaction Design from Carnegie Mellon University, where he also taught interaction design fundamentals.

He lives and works in San Francisco and can be found online at http://www.odannyboy.com and on Twitter at @odannyboy.

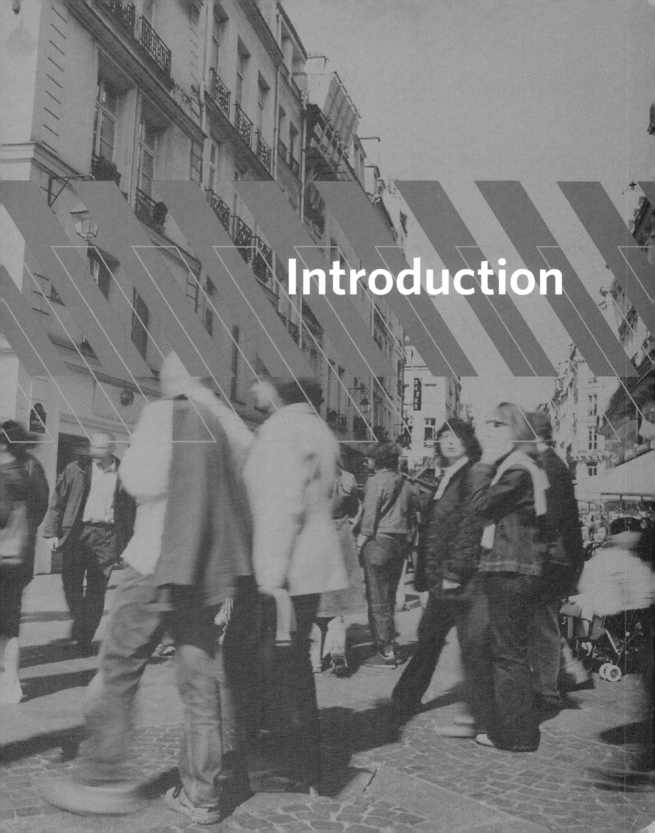

Introduction

In the last decade, and especially in the three years since the first edition of *Designing for Interaction* was published, interaction design as a discipline has come into its own. Even people who have never heard of interaction design—which is to say, most people—understand that how their devices work is as important as how they look. A beautiful mobile phone that functions poorly will cause months of frustration. We know, and the popular press has celebrated, that the best products are those that are functionally—and aesthetically—beautiful.

The past several years have also brought us some absolutely wonderful examples of interaction design that have sparked the imagination: Apple's iPhone, Nintendo's Wii, iRobot's Roomba, Microsoft's Surface, Twitter, and social networks like Facebook. More and more, previously "dumb" products are being outfitted with microprocessors, sensors, and networking capabilities, while the Web has matured to a sophisticated platform for applications of all sorts. Desktop applications have become interwoven with the Internet for interesting combinations. Devices can locate themselves in physical space and provide geo-located information. Exploding processing power, cloud computing, and cheap digital storage make all sorts of new products possible.

All of these things mean the rules of interaction design (such as they are) are being rewritten. The paradigms of how we interact with computing devices, such as the desktop metaphor that we've used for around 40 years now, are changing and being added to. We relate to our products—and thus, to each other—in new ways. It's an exciting time to be in this field.

This book is about the discipline that defines how digital products behave. It doesn't contain any code; indeed, I've tried to be as technology and platform agnostic as possible. I've written this book for both new designers who are just getting started, as well as more advanced designers who might want to refine their processes or add to their set of design tools.

What's New in This Edition

This book addresses a fairly serious flaw in the first edition, namely that while there was a lot of good information, there was no process to help new designers put all that information into an order, into practice. In this edition, Chapters 3 through 8 step through a general design process that can be used for a wide variety of projects. Not every step needs to be followed, and the process is in an ideal order that seldom happens in designing. But at least there is a process.

Additionally, several significant new topics have been added. Design strategy (Chapter 3) is brand new in this edition and I daresay does the best job I've seen in distilling this step (and growing field unto itself) down to its essentials. In the first edition, the translation of research into models and then into concepts was poorly done; this edition addresses that crucial stage. Likewise, there was no mention of design principles, and this was an unfortunate oversight.

Service design, which was its own chapter in the first edition, has been more integrated into the book for two reasons. The first is that service design has become its own area of study. The second reason is that the line between services and products has gotten blurrier. It is difficult to find products, and especially the networked products interaction designers work on, that aren't part of a service of some kind.

Readers of the first edition also asked for references and recommendations to dive deeper into the various topics, so each chapter now has a "For Further Reading" section at the end as well as footnotes to specific articles.

I hope this book is a starting point for your work in interaction design. It is, however, only a book, and books alone can't make you a great designer. Only designing will do that. I urge you to try out everything in this book for yourself, change it as necessary to fit your working style, your company, your users, and the project you're on.

So get to it—there's much to be designed.

San Francisco
June 2009

We become what we behold. We shape our tools, and thereafter our tools shape us.

—Marshall McLuhan

1

What Is Interaction Design?

Every moment of every day, millions of people send e-mail, talk on mobile phones, instant message each other, record TV shows on digital video recorders (DVRs), and listen to music on MP3 players. All of these things are made possible by good engineering. But it's interaction design that makes them usable, useful, and fun.

You benefit from good interaction design every time you:

- Go to an automatic teller machine (ATM) and withdraw cash with a few simple touches on a screen.
- Become engrossed in a computer game.
- Cut and paste cells on a spreadsheet.
- Buy something online.
- Twitter from your mobile phone.
- Update your status on Facebook.

But the reverse is often also true. We suffer from poor interaction design *all around us*. Thousands of interaction design problems wait to be solved—such as when you:

- Try to use the self-checkout at a grocery store and it takes you half an hour.
- Can't get your car to tell you what's wrong with it when it breaks down.
- Wait at a bus stop with no idea when the next bus will arrive.
- Struggle to synchronize your mobile phone to your computer.
- Can't figure out how to set the clock in your microwave oven.

Any time behavior—how a product works—is involved, interaction designers could be involved. Indeed, for the best experience, they *should* be involved.

Back in 1990, Bill Moggridge (**Figure 1.1**), a principal of the design firm IDEO, realized that for some time he and some of his colleagues had been creating a very different kind of design. It wasn't product design exactly, but they were definitely designing products. Nor was it communication design, although they used some of that discipline's tools as well. It wasn't computer science either, although a lot of it had to do with computers and software. No, this was something different. It drew on all those disciplines, but was something else, and it had to do with connecting people through the products they used. Moggridge called this new practice **interaction design**.

In the decades since then, interaction design has grown from a tiny, specialized discipline to one practiced by tens of thousands of people all over the world, many of whom don't call themselves interaction designers and may not even be aware of the discipline. Universities now offer degrees in it, and you'll find practitioners of interaction design at every major software and design firm, as well as in banks such as Wells Fargo, hospitals such as the Mayo Clinic, and appliance manufacturers such as Whirlpool.

Figure 1.1

Bill Moggridge, author of *Designing Interactions* and industrial designer for one of the first laptop computers, the GRiD Compass, coined the term "interaction design" after being talked out of the term "soft-face."

The rise of the commercial Internet in the mid 1990s and the widespread incorporation of microprocessors into machines such as cars, dishwashers, and phones where previously they hadn't been used led to this explosive growth in the number of interaction designers because suddenly a multitude of serious interaction problems needed to be solved. Our gadgets became digital, as did our workplaces, homes, transportation, and communication devices. Our everyday stuff temporarily became unfamiliar to us; the confusion we once collectively had about how to set the clock on the VCR spread to our entire lives. We had to relearn how to dial a phone number and work the stereo and use our computers. It was the initial practitioners of interaction design—mostly coming from other disciplines—who helped us begin to make sense of our newly digitized world and the Internet, and these same people, now aided by new interaction designers, continue to refine and practice the craft as our devices, and our world, grow ever more complex.

What Are Interactions and Interaction Design?

Although we experience examples of good and bad interaction design every day, interaction design as a discipline is tricky to define. In part, this is the result of its interdisciplinary roots: in industrial and communication design, human factors, and human-computer interaction. It's also because a lot of interaction design is invisible, functioning behind the scenes. Why do the Windows and Mac operating systems, which basically do the same thing and can, with some tinkering, even look identical, *feel* so different? Interaction design is about behavior, and behavior is much harder to observe and understand than appearance. It's much easier to notice and discuss a garish color than a subtle transaction that may, over time, drive you crazy.

An interaction, grossly speaking, is a transaction between two entities, typically an exchange of information, but it can also be an exchange of goods or services. This book is called *Designing for Interaction* because it is this sort of exchange that interaction designers try to engender in their work. Interaction designers design *for* the possibility of interaction. The interaction itself takes place between people, machines, and systems, in a variety of combinations.

Three Ways of Looking at Interaction Design

There are three major schools of thought when it comes to defining interaction design:

- A technology-centered view.
- A behaviorist view.
- The Social Interaction Design view.

Figure 1.2

Designed by Marc Andreessen, the Mosaic browser (which eventually evolved into Netscape Navigator) was a fantastic piece of interaction design, making the Web accessible to everyday people. It introduced interaction design paradigms still in use today, such as the back button.

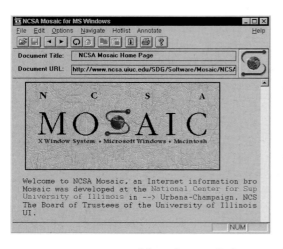

What is common about all three views is that interaction design is seen as an art—an applied art, like furniture making; it's not a science, although some tried and true rules have emerged (see Chapter 7). Interaction design is by its nature contextual: it solves specific problems under a particular set of circumstances using the available materials. For example, even though a 1994 Mosaic browser (**Figure 1.2**) was an excellent piece of interaction design, you wouldn't install it on your computer now. It served its purpose *for its time and context.*

Like other applied arts, such as architecture, interaction design involves many methods and methodologies in its tasks, and ways of working go in and out of vogue and often compete for dominance. Currently, a very user-centered design methodology in which products are generated with users is in style, but this hasn't always been the case, and recently these methods have been challenged (see Chapter 2). Microsoft performs extensive user testing and research; Apple, known for its innovative interaction design, does very little.

The Technology-Centered View

Interaction designers make technology, particularly digital technology, useful, usable, and pleasurable to use. This is why the rise of software and the Internet was also the rise of the field of interaction design. Interaction designers take the raw stuff produced by engineers and programmers and mold it into products that people enjoy using.

The Behaviorist View

As Jodi Forlizzi and Robert Reimann succinctly put it in 1999 in their presentation "Interaction Designers: What we are, what we do, & what we need to know,"[1] interaction design is about "defining the behavior of artifacts, environments, and systems (for example, products)." This view focuses on functionality and feedback: how products behave and provide feedback based on what the people engaged with them are doing.

The Social Interaction Design View

The third, and broadest, view of interaction design is that it is inherently social, revolving around facilitating communication between humans through products. This perspective is sometimes called Social Interaction Design. Technology is nearly irrelevant in this view; any kind of object or device can make a connection between people. These communications can take many forms; they can be one-to-one as with a telephone call, one-to-many as with a blog, or many-to-many as with the stock market.

Why Interaction *Design*?

The term "design" can be difficult to get a handle on. Consider this infamous sentence by design history scholar John Heskett: "Design is to design a design to produce a design."

---

1 Download it online at http://goodgestreet.com/docs/AIGAForlizzi_Reimann2001.pdf

People have many preconceived notions about design, not the least of which is that design concerns only how things look: design as decoration or styling. And while there is nothing wrong with appealing aesthetics, design can be more than that. Communication (graphic) and industrial design bring ways of working that interaction designers embrace as well. Here are some of the approaches that interaction design employs:

Focusing on Users

Designers know that users don't understand or care how the company that makes a product is run and structured. They care about doing their tasks and achieving their goals within their limits. Designers are advocates for end users.

Finding Alternatives

Designing isn't about choosing among multiple options—it's about creating options, finding a "third option" instead of choosing between two undesirable ones. This creation of multiple possible solutions to problems sets designers apart. Consider, for example, Google's AdWords. The company needed advertising for revenue, but users hated traditional banner ads. Thus, designers came up with a third approach: text ads.

Using Ideation and Prototyping

Designers find their solutions through brainstorming and then, most important, building models (**Figure 1.3**) to test the solutions. Certainly, scientists and architects and even accountants model things, but design involves a significant difference: design prototypes aren't fixed. Any particular prototype doesn't necessarily represent *the* solution, only *a* solution. It's not uncommon to use several prototypes to create a single product. Jeff Hawkins, designer of the original PalmPilot, famously carried around small blocks of wood, pretending to write on them and storing them in his shirt pocket until he came upon the right size, shape, and weight for the device.

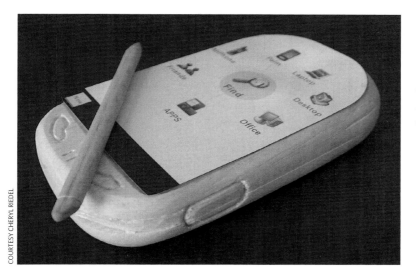

COURTESY CHERYL RIEDEL

Figure 1.3

Interaction designers should plan to create (and throw away) a variety of prototypes of various fidelities to test their concepts.

Collaborating and Addressing Constraints

Few designers work alone. Designers usually need resources (money, materials, developers, printers, and so on) to produce what they dream up, and these resources come with their own constraints. Designers seldom have carte blanche to do whatever they want. They must address business goals, compromise with teammates, and meet deadlines. Designing is almost always a team effort.

Creating Appropriate Solutions

Most designers create solutions that are appropriate only to a particular project at a particular point in time. Designers certainly carry experience and wisdom from one project to the next, but the ultimate solution should uniquely address the issues of that particular problem. This is not to say that the solution (the product) cannot be used in other contexts—experience tells us it can and will be—but that the same exact solution cannot (or shouldn't anyway) be exactly copied for other projects. Amazon has a great e-commerce model, but it can't be exactly replicated elsewhere (although pieces of it certainly can be); it works well within the context of the Amazon site. Design solutions have to be appropriate to the situation.

Drawing on a Wide Range of Influences

Because design touches on so many subject areas (psychology, ergonomics, economics, engineering, architecture, art, and more), designers bring to the table a broad, multidisciplinary spectrum of ideas from which to draw inspiration and solutions.

Incorporating Emotion

In analytical thinking, emotion is seen as an impediment to logic and making the right choices. In design, products without an emotional component are lifeless and do not connect with people. Emotion needs to be thoughtfully included in design decisions. What would the Volkswagen Beetle be without whimsy?

A (Very) Brief History of Interaction Design

There's a tendency to think that interaction design began around the time that Bill Moggridge named it, in 1990, but that's not really true. Interaction design probably began, although obviously not as a formalized discipline, in prerecorded history, when Native Americans and other tribal peoples used smoke signals to communicate over long distances, and the Celts and Inuit used stone markers called cairns or inuksuit as landmarks, to communicate over time (**Figure 1.4**).

Figure 1.4

A modern cairn. In ancient times, cairns were used for many purposes: to mark mountain summits, as directional markers, and as indicators of burial sites.

COURTESY ISTOCKPHOTO

1830s to 1940s

Many centuries later, in the mid 1830s, Samuel Morse created a system to turn simple electromagnetic pulses into a language of sorts and to communicate those words over long distances. Over the next 50 years, Morse code and the telegraph spread across the globe (**Figure 1.5**). Morse not only invented the telegraph, but also the entire system for using it: everything from the electrical systems, to the mechanism for tapping out the code, to the training of telegraph operators. This didn't happen overnight, naturally, but the telegraph was the first instance of communication technology that, unlike the printing press, was too sophisticated for a small number of people to install and use. It required the creators to design an entire system of use.

COURTESY ISTOCKPHOTO

Figure 1.5

Morse code transmitter. The telegraph was the first technology system that wired the world—the so-called "Victorian Internet."

Similarly, other mass communication technologies, from the telephone to radio to television, required engineers to design systems of use and interfaces for the new technologies. And these systems and interfaces were needed not only for the receiving devices—the telephones, radios, and television sets—but also for the devices used to create and send messages: the telephone switches, microphones, television cameras, control booths, and so on. All of these components required interaction design, although it certainly wasn't called that at the time. Indeed, it is very common for the first practitioners of interaction design in any new platform or medium to be the engineers who created the technology itself.

But the machines that fueled these technologies were, for the most part, just that: machines. They responded to human input, certainly, but not in a sophisticated way. They didn't have any awareness that they were being used. For that, we needed computers.

1940s to 1960s

The first wave of computers—ENIAC and its ilk—were engineered, not designed. Humans had to adapt to using them, not vice versa, and this meant speaking the machines' language, not ours. Entering anything into the computer required days plugging in cables or, in later machines, hours preparing statements on punch cards or paper tape for the machine to read. These paper slips were the interface (**Figure 1.6**). Engineers expended very little design effort to make the early computers more usable. Instead, they worked to make them faster and more powerful, so the computers could solve complicated computational problems.

At the same time as these developments were occurring in the computing field, other disciplines that eventually informed interaction design were

Figure 1.6

Punch cards—one of the first interfaces with computers, as well as a means of data storage. By the 1980s, almost all of them had been phased out by command-line or GUI interfaces.

COURTESY ISTOCKPHOTO

growing, too. Engineers and industrial designers such as Henry Dreyfuss created the new field of human factors, which focused on the design of products for different sizes and shapes of people. The field of ergonomics focused on workers' productivity and safety, determining the best ways to perform tasks. Cognitive psychology, focusing on human learning and problem solving, experienced a resurgence, led by such academics as Allen Newell and George Miller.

In 1945, *Atlantic Monthly* published a seminal article titled "As We May Think"[2] (reportedly written in 1936) by Vannevar Bush, in which he introduced the Memex, a microfilm-based device for storing books, records, and communications, which is mechanized so that it may be consulted with exceeding speed and flexibility.

It consists of a desk, and while it can presumably be operated from a distance, it is primarily a piece of furniture. On the top are slanting translucent screens, on which material can be projected for convenient reading. There is a keyboard, and sets of buttons and levers. Otherwise it looks like an ordinary desk.

The Memex (**Figure 1.7**) was Bush's concept for augmenting human memory. While just a concept, it was the first imagining of hypertext, and one of the first for a desktop computing system. It has influenced generations of interaction designers since, starting with Douglas Engelbart and Ted Nelson in the 1960s.

Figure 1.7

One of the drawings of Vannevar Bush's Memex device as it appeared in *Life* magazine in 1945. Note the stylus—an input device decades ahead of its time.

1960s to 1970s

As computers became more powerful, engineers began to focus on the people using computers in the 1960s, and began to devise new methods of input and new uses for the machines. Engineers added control panels to the front of computers, allowing input through a complicated series of switches, usually in combination with a set of punch cards that were processed as a group (batch processing).

---

[2] Read it online at http://www.theatlantic.com/doc/194507/bush

In 1960, Ted Nelson started his Project Xanadu, with the goal of creating computer networks with simple user interfaces. While it never really came to fruition, it was the first attempt at a hypertext system. Nelson, in fact, coined the term "hypertext" in 1963.

Figure 1.8

Ivan Sutherland's
Sketchpad. One
of Sketchpad's
innovations was
master drawings of
which users could
create duplicates.
If the user changed
the master drawing,
all the instances of
the drawing would
change as well.

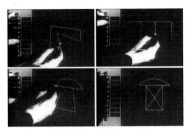

1963 also brought Ivan Sutherland's Sketchpad (**Figure 1.8**), the first computer program to utilize a fully graphical user interface and a light pen for input. Using Sketchpad, users could draw both horizontal and vertical lines and combine them into figures and shapes. Sutherland in 1968 created The Sword of Damocles, which is widely considered to be the first virtual reality system. (The head-mounted display worn by the user was so heavy it had to be suspended from the ceiling, thus inspiring the name.)

Sometime around 1965, the first "killer application," e-mail, was invented as a way for multiple users of a time-sharing mainframe computer to communicate. By 1966, e-mail had expanded to allow users to send messages between different computers. By 1971, e-mail was being sent across ARPANET, the precursor to the Internet. Ray Tomlinson, who created the e-mail standards still in use (such as the @ symbol in e-mail addresses), sent the first e-mail between different host systems, reportedly something insignificant like "QWERTYUIOP."

The ARPANET (Advanced Research Projects Agency Network) was developed by ARPA of the United States Department of Defense and was the predecessor of the global Internet. Conceived as the "Intergalactic Computer Network" in 1962 by J.C.R. Licklider, the first two links of the network (UCLA and Stanford) connected on November 21, 1969. While ARPANET certainly wasn't a design milestone, its creation lead to the platform and medium that caused interaction design to flourish: the Internet.

In 1968, Doug Engelbart did a 90-minute presentation that is now known as "The Mother of All Demos"[3] (**Figure 1.9**). In it, Engelbart showed the work he'd been doing for the previous several years, essentially creating the next two decades of interaction design. As well as being the first public

---

3 Watch it online at http://sloan.stanford.edu/MouseSite/1968Demo.html

demonstration of the mouse, Engelbart demonstrated an incredible variety of interaction design paradigms we now take for granted, such as point and click, hyperlinks, cutting and pasting, and networked collaboration.

Figure 1.9

December 9, 1968, was Doug Engelbart's "Mother of All Demos" at the Fall Joint Computer Conference in San Francisco. Engelbart demonstrated a mouse, video conferencing, e-mail, and hypertext on the NLS (oNLine System) to 1,000 attendees.

Many of these paradigms were to find a home at Xerox PARC (Palo Alto Research Center), founded in 1970. The head of Xerox PARC, Bob Taylor, urged employees to think of computers not as just processing devices, but instead as communication devices.

COURTESY MARCIN WICHARY

Xerox PARC remains legendary. Its contributions to the field, many of which are contained in its signature products the Xerox Alto (**Figure 1.10**) and the Xerox Star, are everything from windowing and icons and the desktop metaphor to WYSIWYG text editing. Employees included Alan Kay, who conceived of the first laptop computer, the Dynabook, in 1968; Larry Tesler and Tim Mott, who conceived of the desktop metaphor and such now-standard interactions as cut-and-paste; and Robert Metcalfe, who invented Ethernet networking in 1973.

Figure 1.10

Xerox Alto. One of the first personal computers, and the first to use the desktop metaphor.

Famously, Steve Jobs got a demo of the Xerox Star and proceeded to include its innovations into Apple's subsequent computers, the Lisa and, eventually, the Macintosh.

In the mid-to-late 1970s, experiments like Myron Krueger's VIDEOPLACE explored virtual reality experiences and gestural interfaces, and the first touchscreen devices became commercially available.

The 1970s also began the computer gaming industry with games such as Pong (1972) and the Atari 2600 gaming console (1977). This reflected another major trend in the 1970s: the shifting focus from the computer itself—the hardware—to the software that runs it, particularly software that was not designed by computer scientists and engineers for themselves or trained operators. Designers and engineers in the 1970s refined and expanded the command-line interface (which had begun in the 1950s) into such industry-defining software, as VisiCalc, the first spreadsheet software, introduced in 1979, and WordStar, a popular word-processing program introduced in 1978 (**Figure 1.11**).

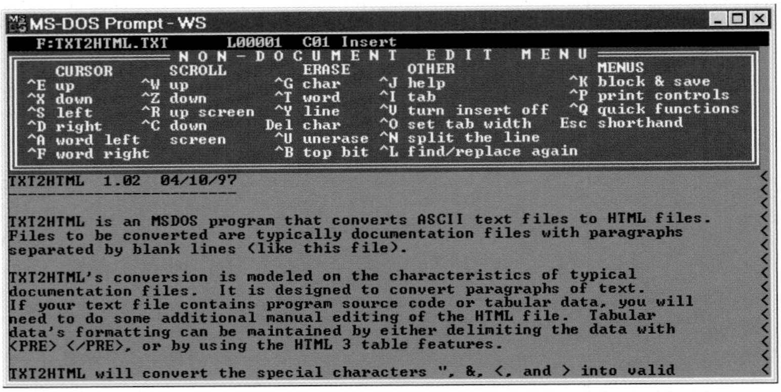

Figure 1.11

WordStar and its ilk were some of the first pieces of commercial software that weren't designed by programmers for programmers. WordStar dominated the word processing market from its release in 1978 until the early 1990s, when it was surpassed by Microsoft Word.

1980s

This new emphasis on users came to fruition in the early 1980s with the explosion of the graphical user interface—spearheaded by Apple Computer, first in the Lisa (**Figure 1.12**) and then in the Macintosh—to a mass audience. Like at Xerox PARC, the interaction design of the Lisa and Macintosh was a group effort, featuring designers such as Joy Mountford, Jef Raskin, and Bill Atkinson.

The 1980s was the era of the personal computer. For the first time, most people working with computing devices were working with their own, and thus had a more one-to-one relationship with one than in previous decades. 1981 also saw some of the first portable computers, such as the Osborne 1. The increasing memory and power of the devices allowed for more sophisticated software such as Mitch Kapor's Lotus 1-2-3 (1983).

COURTESY MARCIN WICHARY

Figure 1.12

Apple Lisa was a precursor (of sorts) to the Macintosh, although more powerful and, in many ways, more advanced. It was, however, a commercial failure.

This increasing sophistication and power was demonstrated most capably in the surge of so-called "video" or "arcade" games. Gaming consoles such as the Sega Genesis (1989) and the Super Nintendo Entertainment System (1990) brought unprecedented graphics and computing power to a mass audience. This era also featured game designers such as the legendary Shigeru Miyamoto, the "Father of Modern Video Games" and creator of Mario, Legend of Zelda, and Donkey Kong. Gaming provided a new set of parallel interaction design paradigms that exist alongside the more "traditional" or "professional" ones for the desktop. (Mobile and touchscreen devices are other similar parallel tracks.)

In the mid-1980s, bulletin board systems (BBSs) like The WELL (1985) and Prodigy (1988) sprung up so that people could leave e-mail and messages for one another on remote computers using dial-up modems.

In the late 1980s, Mark Weiser and John Seely Brown at Xerox PARC began putting together the frameworks and definitions for what would become known as ubiquitous computing, or **ubicomp**. It's taken about two decades, but the era of ubicomp has likely already begun (see Chapter 9).

1990s

The era of networked computing, and the beginning of interaction design as a formal discipline, began in earnest during the 1990s. The World Wide Web, which allowed anyone to easily publish hypertext documents accessible to anyone with a modem worldwide, and the mass adoption of e-mail, brought the need for better interaction design to the forefront. Marc Andreessen's Mosaic browser (1993) was an important piece of interaction design, introducing such paradigms as the back button.

It is no exaggeration to state that the advent of the commercial, public Internet changed the world and the relationship of humans to computing devices and even to information. The early Web was as much a sandbox for new interactions as was the desktop a decade before, if not more so. The Web, along with technologies such as Adobe's Flash, allowed for experimentation on a grand scale, and for a time, everything—including general controls like scrollbars and buttons—were up for grabs. Eventually, in the late 1990s, standards began to emerge and the Web stabilized as a platform.

At the same time, engineers and designers began building sensors and microprocessors, which were getting smaller, cheaper, and more powerful, into things that weren't considered computers: cars, appliances, and electronic equipment. Suddenly, these physical objects could demonstrate kinds of behavior that they previously couldn't; they could display an "awareness" of their environment and of how they were being used that was previously inconceivable. Cars could monitor their own engines and alert drivers to problems before they occurred. Stereos could adjust their settings based on the type of music being played. Dishwashers could lengthen their wash cycles depending on how dirty the dishes were. All these behaviors needed to be designed and, most important, communicated to the human beings using the objects.

Other pieces of technology facilitated interactions among people, mostly in the entertainment space. Karaoke spread from bars in China and Japan to the United States (**Figure 1.13**). Arcade video games like Dance Dance Revolution allowed expression in front of crowds. Multiplayer games on computers and game consoles like the Sony PlayStation facilitated competition and collaboration in new ways. Online communities like EverQuest and The Sims Online incorporated sophisticated economies that rivaled those of offline countries.

COURTESY ISTOCKPHOTO

Figure 1.13

Although the butt
of jokes in the US,
the karaoke machine
is a surprisingly
rich example of
interaction design.
It provides a way
to communicate
emotionally with
friends.

Mobile phones and devices—which had existed since the 1980s—enjoyed explosive market growth in the 1990s. Today, billions of customers carry these devices with them. Starting as simply a means of making calls on the go, mobile phones can now contain myriad digital features that rival those of desktop computers. Personal digital assistants (PDAs) got off to a shaky start with the failure of Apple's Newton in 1995, but by the end of the decade, they had gained traction with devices like the PalmPilot and BlackBerry PDAs.

2000s to Present

The turn of the millennium also coincided with the era of social software and the beginning of the era of ubiquitous computing. No longer did many people have a one-to-one relationship with devices, but instead had access to many devices able to interact with each other and the Internet over a network. By 2003, laptops had started outselling desktop systems. As of this writing (2009), nearly as many people access the Web via a mobile device as with a traditional desktop or laptop, and that number is likely to be surpassed shortly.

As the Internet matured, so did the technologies creating and driving it. Since the end of the 1990s, the Internet has become less about reading content than about doing things: executing stock trades, making new (and

Figure 1.14

Skype takes a familiar paradigm, the buddy list from instant messaging, and couples it with a new technology, Voice over IP (VoIP), in order to make phone calls via the Internet.

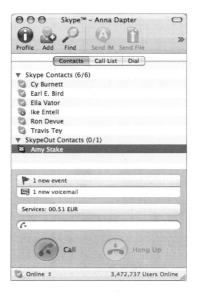

finding old) acquaintances, selling items, manipulating live data, sharing photos, making personal connections between one piece of content and another. The Internet also provides several new ways of communicating, among them instant messaging, Voice over Internet Protocol (VoIP) (**Figure 1.14**), and Twitter.

The Internet has become a platform for applications, in much the same way that Microsoft DOS once was, but these applications can take advantage of the many features of the Internet: collective actions like the SETI@Home project in which people compete to see who can find extraterrestrial activity first, data that is collected passively from large numbers of people as with Amazon's "People who bought this also bought..." feature, far-flung social communities such as that of online photography site Flickr, aggregation of many sources of data in XML and RSS feeds, near real-time access to timely data like stock quotes and news, and easy sharing of content such as blogs and YouTube.

Access to the Internet, through broadband connections and wireless networks on portable devices, is changing the types of interactions we can have and where we can have them. Our cities and towns are becoming platforms and data sources for geo-located services. Services themselves are being affected by interaction design (see "Products and Services" later in this chapter).

Gestural interfaces and touchscreen devices such as Nintendo's Wii and Apple's iPhone have ushered in a new era of interaction design, where taps on a screen or gestures in space are becoming a new set of commands for our devices.

There's never been a better time to be an interaction designer. The discipline's future (see Chapter 9) contains both many challenges and many possibilities.

Marc Rettig on Interaction Design's History and Future

Marc Rettig is a designer, educator, and researcher, as well as founder and principal of Fit Associates. He has taught at Carnegie Mellon's Graduate School of Design (where he held the 2003 Nierenberg Distinguished Chair of Design) and the Institute of Design, IIT, in Chicago. Marc served as chief experience officer of the user experience firm HannaHodge, and was a director of user experience at Cambridge Technology Partners.

When does the history of interaction design begin?

I'll pick the work at Xerox PARC on the Star interface as a very early example of self-conscious interaction design, the publication of which influenced others to begin working in a similar way. As just one example, the idea of associating a program with a picture was born there. We call them icons, and forget what a breakthrough connection between interface element and underlying meaning that once was. That was the early-to-mid 1970s, and the Star papers are still great reading.

What fields have had the greatest influence on interaction design?

As it is currently practiced? Well, software development and graphic design. To some extent, industrial design. A dab of psychology and human factors. A dab of business.

What I imagine we need more of: filmmaking and theater, biology, counseling and therapy (the professionals at acquiring and checking an empathetic point of view), maybe anthropology. And especially linguistics—some new branch of linguistics that nobody is yet carving out: the linguistics of designed interactions.

What can interaction designers learn from noninteractive tools?

I'd like to spin the question slightly by observing that to an interaction designer, watching a tool in use is the same as observing a conversation. Everything, in a sense, has its inputs and outputs. From that point of view, the boundary between "interactive" and "noninteractive" tools starts to dissolve.

Interaction design is largely about the meaning that people assign to things and events, and how people try to express meanings. So to learn from any tool, interactive or not, go watch

Marc Rettig on Interaction Design's History and Future *(continued)*

people using it. You'll hear them talk to the tool. You'll see them assign all sorts of surprising interpretations to shapes, colors, positioning, dings, dents, and behaviors. You'll see them fall in love with a thing as it becomes elegantly worn. You'll see them come to hate a thing and choose to ignore it, sell it, or even smash it. And I guarantee you won't have to do much of this before you encounter someone who makes a mental mapping you would never dream possible. And you'll learn from that.

I've been using tea kettles as an example in some of my teaching, because on the one hand kettles are so familiar to us, and they're only interactive in a borderline, predictable, mechanical sort of way. But once you start to examine the meanings involved with kettles in use, you realize they have things to say that people would love to know, but most designs don't allow them to be said. "I'm getting hot, but I have no water in me." "My water is a good temperature for a child's cocoa." "I'm too hot to touch." "I need to be cleaned." And so on. I'd love the chance to take a serious interaction design approach to something like a tea kettle.

A Stew of Disciplines

Interaction design as a formal discipline has been around for less than two decades. It's a young field, still defining itself and figuring out its place among sister disciplines such as information architecture (IA), industrial design (ID), visual (or graphic) design, user experience (UX) design, and human factors. In addition, some of these other disciplines are also new and still discovering their boundaries as well, or are radically changing to accommodate changing design landscape. **Figure 1.15** attempts to clarify the relationships between them.

As you can see, most of the disciplines fall at least partially under the umbrella of user-experience design, the discipline of looking at all aspects—visual design, interaction design, sound design, and so on—of the user's encounter with a product, and making sure they are in harmony.

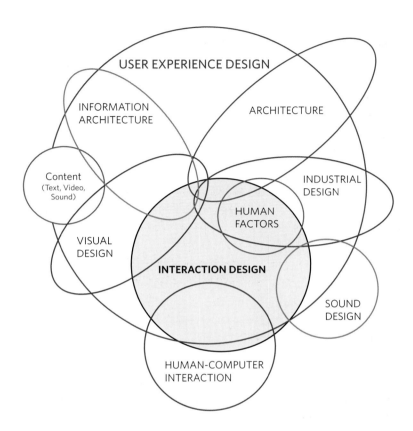

Figure 1.15

The disciplines
surrounding
interaction design.

Information architecture is concerned with the structure of content: how
to best organize and label content so that users find the information they
need. Yahoo, with its dozens of labeled and categorized content areas, offers
an excellent illustration of information architecture. Visual design is about
creating a visual language to communicate content. The fonts, colors, and
layout of user interfaces and printed materials like this book provide examples of visual design. Industrial design is about form—shaping objects in a
way that communicates their use while also making them functional. Physical objects like furniture, kitchenware, and mechanical objects illustrate
industrial design. Human factors ensure our products conform to the limitations of the human body, both physically and psychologically. Human-
computer interaction is closely related to interaction design, but its methods
are more quantitative, and its methods are more those of engineering and

computer science than of design. Architecture concerns itself with physical spaces: their form and use ("program"). Sound design defines a set of noises, spoken word, or music to create an aural landscape.

It's easy to see why people are confused!

Although these disciplines are separate, as the figure illustrates, they still overlap a great deal. In fact, where the disciplines overlap can be major areas of practice, such as interface design, where visual and interaction design meet; or navigation, where visual and interaction design meet information architecture.

The best products involve multiple disciplines working in harmony. What is a laptop computer except a blend of the fruits of many of these disciplines? Separating them can be nearly impossible.

You'll also notice that many of these disciplines have parts that lie outside the user experience realm. This is because many of these disciplines have tasks that have to do with getting their designs produced, developed, and built, and those tasks may have little to do with what the user experiences.

It is also important to note that not every organization needs a specialist working in each discipline; within an organization, one person, who might be called anything from an information architect to a user-interface engineer, can—and probably will—shift back and forth as needs require. It's the role that is important, not the title. The "imagineer" at Disney might do a job similar to that of the "user-interface architect" at a startup company.

Case Study: Microsoft Office 2007

The Company

Microsoft, the world's largest software company.

The Problem

In the early 2000s, it was clear to many inside Microsoft that something had to be done about their best-selling, nearly ubiquitous software suite Microsoft Office. The original interaction and interface design, created a decade before, was not scaling well. New features were being hidden by the interface, and even features users had requested and had been put into new versions of the product couldn't be found by those very same users. The software appeared bloated, inefficient, and unwieldy. For example, 50 menu items and 2 toolbars from Microsoft Word 1.0 had ballooned to 260 menu items and over 30 toolbars by Word 2003.

Case Study: Microsoft Office 2007 *(continued)*

The Process

The Microsoft design team started by analyzing anonymous data collected about how people were using Office 2003. They looked for two important things: desirable features with low usage numbers (which meant people couldn't find them) and frequently-used features that were hard to get to (which meant people really wanted them). They focused on the design principle (see Chapter 6) "Use of a broader set of tools" and did several years of iterative prototyping to come up with a new set of interaction design paradigms for users.

The Solution

Microsoft Office 2007 has literally 1000 enhancements to it, all of which take up less screen space than previous versions. One main (and controversial) UI change was the Ribbon (pictured), which clusters pieces of functionality at the top of the screen in large, easy-to-click targets. Another innovation was known as "the Minibar," which appeared near objects that were highlighted and allowed users to quickly modify the selection without having to fiddle with menus or the Ribbon. The new design has been a best-seller, and the headline for the review in the *New York Times* read "From Bloated to Sleek."

Products and Services

Interaction designers work on a wide variety of products: everything from Web sites to desktop software, from consumer electronics to robots, from mobile and medical devices to interactive environments. These products can be solely digital (software) or mostly analog (robots), physical (appliances) or incorporeal (a gestural interface), or some combination thereof.

Since behaviors, technology platforms, and media frequently change, good interaction design doesn't align itself to anyone in particular. Interaction design should be technologically agnostic, concerned only with the right technologies for the task at hand, be it a complex software application or a simple sign.

More and more, the products that interaction designers work on are connected to a service, to the point where it may not be meaningful to distinguish between them anymore for interaction design. A *service* is a chain of sequential, parallel, or nonlinear activities or events that form a process and have value for the end user. You engage in a service when you get your shoes shined or your nails manicured or when you visit a fast-food restaurant. Your mobile phone's usage plan is a service, and you participate in a service every time you travel on a plane, train, or taxi. Services can be small and discreet, such as the sale of postage stamps by some ATM machines, or they can be huge, such as the sorting and delivery of physical mail. Service providers are all around us and account for an enormous portion of the world economy— from restaurants and bars to dry cleaners, hospitals, construction companies, street cleaners, and even complete governments. Services are everywhere.

Services greatly affect our quality of life because we are touched by so many of them every day. A poor service can make your subway ride to work uncomfortable, your packages late or undelivered, your lunch distasteful, your mobile phone coverage poor, and your ability to find evening TV shows problematic.

Shelley Evenson on Service Design

Shelley Evenson is an associate professor and director of graduate studies at Carnegie Mellon University's School of Design. Prior to her academic career, she was vice president and chief experience strategist for Scient, director of design at DKA/Digital Knowledge Assets, director at Doblin Group, and vice president of Fitch. She has published a number of articles and presented papers at numerous conferences on design languages in hypermedia, interaction design, design research, and service design.

Why is service design important?

According to one IBM report, today more than 70 percent of the U.S. labor force is engaged in service delivery. New technology has enabled internationally tradable services. We are at a tipping point. A huge portion of the economy is now focused on knowledge-based information services. I believe that as we shift to this service-centered society, it won't be good enough to view services from a purely management or operations-based perspective. Companies will need to turn to service design and innovation to differentiate themselves in increasingly competitive markets and to create opportunities that address new challenges in the service sector.

How is designing a service different from designing a product?

When designing a product, much of the focus is on mediating the interaction between the person and the artifact. Great product designers consider more of the context in their design. In service design, designers must create resources that connect people to people, people to machines, and machines to machines. You must consider the environment, the channel, the touchpoint. Designing for service becomes a systems problem and often even a systems challenge. The elements or resources that designers need to create to mediate the interactions must work on all these levels and at the same time facilitate connections that are deeply personal, open to participation and change, and drop-dead stunning.

Shelley Evenson on Service Design *(continued)*

What can interaction designers bring to the design of services?

Interaction designers use methods in their process that can be directly applied to service design. Immersive ethnographic methods can help designers account for the complexity of service elements that are onstage, backstage, visible, and invisible in the service experience. We add a kind of theater or enactment to our service process. Enactment is when first the development team and then participants from the delivery organization act out the service experience with specific roles and rough props. I've seen this technique become more popular with interaction designers in recent days. Developing constituent archetypes or personas is also useful in service design since the characters can be used to drive service scenarios before they are enacted. Nearly all the methods introduced in this book could apply.

What fields are most in need of service design right now?

I believe there are loads of opportunity in health care. The model for service delivery hasn't changed much in the last 50 years. Medical research and technology have advanced beyond what the model can account for. Additionally, people's expectations for service have changed. Today we have endless access to information, self-service everything, and overnight delivery. These new expectations are finally hitting the medical profession. Some institutions are responding, most notably the Mayo Clinic and UPMC.

Another area of opportunity is software. I think people are just beginning to look beyond the metaphor of software as product, to seeing the potential of product/service systems, or even systems of systems, as new means of framing company offerings. Financial services are another area of opportunity.

Where do you see service design headed in the near future?

Europeans have been seriously thinking about service design for over 10 years. They've made a lot of progress, especially with regard to designing for service experiences that encourage more responsible product ownership and sustainable lifestyles. We could begin to see some of those efforts cross over to the U.S.

I also believe we will begin to see more business strategists looking forward toward experience in designing for service instead of backward toward products. When this happens, we may see a demand for service designers that rivals what happened for interaction designers in the Internet boom days.

Whether it is a Web site, a device that plugs into a network, a robot, or an interactive environment, it is likely most of the products interaction designers work on will live in some sort of service, so it can be useful to have a holistic, service design mentality when working on a product.

> NOTE   *Throughout this book, the outcome of the design process will be called a "product" even though in some cases, that product may be a complete service or (more likely) part of a service.*

Why Practice Interaction Design?

In poem after poem, the late barfly poet extraordinaire Charles Bukowski noted that it wasn't the big things that drove people mad, it was the small stuff: little things not going well, small irritants that over time made you crazy—the leaking faucet, the stains that won't come out of clothes, the mobile phone that won't dial. Interaction designers try to ameliorate some of that annoyance, making sure that the products and services people deal with make sense, are usable and useful, and are even engaging and fun. Some of what good interaction designers do is make the world better by removing those little irritants in life, some of which we don't know exist until they are gone.

Humans have an amazing tendency to become accustomed to the terrible, inconvenient, and awkward. We can live with horrible situations for long periods until something better comes along, something we may not have even known we needed. Take the telephone, for instance. For decades, all calls had to be routed through a human operator, who (if she or he felt like it) could also listen in on your call (**Figure 1.16**). Dial phones weren't introduced until 1919, and it wasn't until the 1950s—80 years after the phone was invented—that direct distance dialing (DDD) allowed callers to dial long-distance without the help of an operator. The last manual phones weren't phased out until the 1970s—almost a hundred years after they were introduced!

COURTESY ISTOCKPHOTO

Figure 1.16

Old telephone exchange. Imagine all your long-distance calls being routed through this. Now imagine having to operate it for long periods of time.

But interaction design isn't only about fixing problems; it's also about invention, about creating new products, and by doing so, making the world a better place to live. The Internet would be a collection of servers and wires without Web browsers, e-mail clients, Twitter, games, blogging tools, social networking sites, and instant messaging and VoIP programs. These products—these designed products—allow us to connect with one another through time and space, like the smoke signals and cairns of our ancient ancestors.

It's easy to forget in the middle of a harrowing project, but the work that interaction designers do matters in profound ways. Interaction designers change the world, a little at a time, through the products they create.

For Further Reading

Designing Interactions, Bill Moggridge

Hackers, Steven Levy

Where Wizards Stay Up Late, Katie Hafner

Dealers in Lightning: Xerox PARC and the Dawning of the Computer Age, Michael Hiltzik

The Victorian Internet, Tom Standage

Geeks Bearing Gifts: How the Computer World Got This Way, Ted Nelson

The Dream Machine: J.C.R. Licklider and the Revolution That Made Computing Personal, M. Mitchell Waldrop

2

The Four
Approaches to
Interaction Design

In the field of interaction design, not only are there different schools of thought about what interaction design is (see Chapter 1), but there are also different styles of working that should be examined.

There are four major approaches to tackling interaction design projects:

▶   User-centered design (UCD)

▶   Activity-centered design

▶   Systems design

▶   Genius design

All four have been used to create successful products, and it is typically up to designers to select (sometimes unconsciously) the way that works best for them. A few assertions apply to all these approaches:

▶   They can be used in many different situations to create vastly different products and services, from Web sites to consumer electronics to interactive environments.

▶   Most problematic situations can be improved by deploying at least one of these approaches to solving the problem.

▶   The best designers are those who can move between approaches, applying the best approach to the situation, sometimes applying multiple approaches even within a single project.

▶   An individual designer will probably gravitate toward one of these approaches more than others. Some of these approaches may feel simply wrong. Designers will probably generally work with the approaches they feel most comfortable employing. At different times, however, another approach may be the best way to solve a design problem, so it is important that interaction designers know all four approaches.

Table 2.1 provides a quick comparison of the four approaches.

We'll look in detail at each of these approaches, outlining in broad strokes the philosophy behind each one in its purest form (which is unlikely to be found in practice). We'll start with the approach that is currently the most popular: user-centered design.

TABLE 2.1 Four Approaches to Design

Approach	Overview	Users	Designer
User-centered design	Focus on user needs and goals	The guides of design	Translator of user needs and goals
Activity-centered design	Focus on the tasks and activities that need to be accomplished	Performers of the activities	Creates tools for actions
Systems design	Focus on the components of a system	Set the goals of the system	Makes sure all the parts of the system are in place
Genius design	Skill and wisdom of designers used to make products	Source of validation	The source of inspiration

User-Centered Design

The philosophy behind user-centered design is simply this: users know best. The people who will be using a product or service know what their needs, goals, and preferences are, and it is up to the designer to find out those things and design for them. One shouldn't design a service for selling coffee without first talking to coffee drinkers. Designers, however well-meaning, aren't the users. Designers are involved simply to facilitate the achievement of the users' goals. Participation from users is sought (ideally) at every stage of the design process. Indeed, some designers view users as co-creators.

The concept of user-centered design has been around for a long time; its roots are in industrial design and ergonomics and in the belief that designers should try to fit products to people instead of the other way around. Industrial designer Henry Dreyfuss, who designed the iconic 500 series telephone for Bell Telephones, first popularized the method with his 1955 book *Designing for People*. But while industrial designers remembered this legacy, software engineers were blissfully unaware of it, and for decades they churned out software that made sense in terms of the way computers work, but not in terms of the way that people work. To be fair, this focus was not all the engineers' fault; with the limited processing speed and memory of computers for the first 40 years of their existence, it's sometimes astounding that engineers could make computers useful at all. The constraints of the system were huge. There was little concern for the user because it took so much effort and development time simply to get the computer to work correctly.

In the 1980s, designers and computer scientists working in the new field of human-computer interaction began questioning the practice of letting engineers design the interface for computer systems. Increased memory, processing speed, and color monitors now made, different types of interfaces possible, and a movement began to focus the design of computer software around users, not around computers. This movement became known as user-centered design (UCD).

Goals are really important in UCD; designers focus on what the user ultimately wants to accomplish. The designer then determines the tasks and means necessary to achieve those goals, but always with the users' needs and preferences in mind.

In the best (or at least most thorough) UCD approach, designers involve users in every stage of the project. Designers consult users (and potential users) at the beginning of the project to see if the proposed project will even address the users' needs. Designers conduct extensive research (see Chapter 4) up front to determine what the users' goals are in the current situation. Then, as designers begin ideation (see Chapter 6), users are brought in to help generate concepts (which is known as **participatory design**). Designers (often alongside usability professionals) evaluate and test prototypes with users as well (see Chapter 8).

Simply put, throughout the project, user data is the determining factor in making design decisions. When a question arises as to how something should be done, the users' wants and needs determine the response. For example, if during user research for an e-commerce Web site, users say they want the shopping cart in the upper-right corner of the page, when the shopping cart is ultimately positioned on the page, that's likely where the shopping cart will be.

User goals—the real target of UCD—are notoriously slippery and often hard to define, especially long-term goals. Or else they are so vague, it is nearly impossible to design for them. Let's say a designer is creating an application to help college students manage their schedules. What's the goal there? To help students do better in school? But why? So they can graduate?

What's the goal there? To get a good job? To become educated? User goals can quickly become like Russian dolls, with goals nested inside goals.

That being said, what UCD is best at is getting designers to move away from their own preferences and instead to focus on the needs and goals of the users, and this result should not be undervalued. Designers, like everyone else, carry around their own experiences and prejudices, and those can conflict with what users require in a product or service. A UCD approach removes designers from that trap. "You are not the user" is a mantra often espoused by UCD designers.

UCD doesn't always work, however. Relying on users for all design insights can sometimes result in a product or service that is too narrowly focused. Designers may, for instance, be basing their work on the wrong set or type of users. For products that will be used by millions of people, UCD may simply be impractical because the audience is too segmented. UCD is a valuable approach, but it is only one approach to designing.

Activity-Centered Design

Activity-centered design (ACD) doesn't focus on the goals and preferences of users, but instead on behavior surrounding particular tasks. Activities can be loosely defined as a cluster of actions and decisions that are done for a purpose. Activities can be brief and simple (making a sandwich) or time consuming and involved (learning a foreign language). Activities can take moments or years. You can do them alone or with others, as is the case, for example, when you sing a song. Some activities, such as withdrawing money from an ATM, have a set ending—in this case, getting the money. Others, such as listening to music, have no fixed ending. The activity simply stops when the actor (or some outside force) decides it is over.

ACD has its roots in activity theory, which is a psychological framework from the first half of the 20th century. Activity theory posits that people create tools as a result of "exteriorized" mental processes. Decision-making and interior life of individuals are de-emphasized in favor of *what people do* and the tools they collectively create in order to make (and to communicate). This philosophy translates well into activity-centered design, where the activity and the tools to support it—not the user—are at the center of the design process.

Figure 2.1

A cello is a product
that was definitely
designed using
activity-centered
design. A UCD
designer would have
likely thought it far
too hard to learn.

COURTESY ISTOCKPHOTO

Many of the products we use today
were designed using activity-centered
design, especially functional tools like
appliances and cars. Activity-centered
design allows designers to tightly focus
on the work at hand and create support for the activity itself, instead of for
more distant goals (**Figure 2.1**). Thus,
it's well-suited for complicated actions
or for products with varied and large
amounts of users.

The *purpose* of an activity is not necessarily a *goal*. Purposes are generally
more focused and tangible than goals.
Take the activity of raking leaves, for
example. The gardener might have a goal (to have a tidy yard) but the purpose
of raking is simple: to collect leaves. ACD would focus on collecting leaves.

Of course, sometimes goals and purposes can be the same or similar. For
example, in the activity of making tea, the goal and the purpose are pretty
much the same: to drink tea. Few people have as a goal to become a master
tea brewer.

Activities are made up of actions and decisions, otherwise known as *tasks*.
Tasks can be as discrete as pushing a button or as complicated as performing all the steps necessary to launch a nuclear missile. The purpose of tasks
is to engage in (and possibly complete) an activity. Each task is a moment in
the life of the activity, and many of those moments can be aided by design.
For example, a button can be provided to turn a device on, and a label or
instructions may aid a user in making a decision.

The difference between a task and an activity can be fairly minor. Some
tasks have enough parts to them to be considered subactivities unto themselves. For example, in making a phone call, one of the tasks is finding the
right number to dial. There are quite a few ways to find a phone number: call
a service for assistance, look up the number in the phone or online, recall
it from memory, and so on. Each of these solutions to the task of finding a
number is itself a task. So is finding a phone number a task or an activity?

For designers, the difference is usually academic; it has to be designed for no matter what it's called.

Like user-centered design, activity-centered design relies on research as the basis for its insights, albeit differently. Designers observe and interview users for insights about their behavior more than about their goals and motivations. Designers catalog users' activities and tasks, perhaps add some missing tasks, and then design solutions to help users accomplish the task, not achieve a goal per se.

Ultimately, activity-centered design allows designers to focus narrowly on the tasks at hand and design products and tools that support those tasks. The task "submit form" will probably require a button. The task "turn device on" will probably require a switch or button. And so on. The activity, not necessarily the people doing the activity, guides the design.

Activity-centered design can be ethically tricky. Some tasks require skill—sometimes great skill—and designers shouldn't ignore this in designing alternatives. Removing or automating people's valuable skills is morally troubling. It may take weeks to learn a call-center's software, for instance, and removing the need for that skill can devalue employees. But then again, perhaps the reason the software takes weeks to learn is because it's poorly designed. Designers should be especially careful of the tasks they automate: it is very easy to de-skill users, to remove tasks that may be tedious or difficult to learn, but are also pleasurable to perform. Imagine being asked to design a piano that was easier to learn and play!

Another danger in activity-centered design is that by fixating on tasks, designers won't look for solutions for the problem as a whole. They won't see the forest for the trees. There's an old design adage: you'll get a different result if you set out to design a vase instead of something to hold flowers. By focusing on small tasks, designers can find themselves designing vase after vase and never a hanging garden.

Systems Design

Systems design is a very analytical way of approaching design problems; it uses an established arrangement of components to create design solutions. Whereas in user-centered design, the user is at the center of the design process, here a system—a set of entities that act upon each other—is. A system isn't necessarily a computer, although it can be. Systems can also consist of people, devices, machines, and objects. Systems can range from the simple (the heating system in your house) to enormously complex (whole governments). Systems design is a structured, rigorous design approach that is excellent for tackling complex problems and offers a holistic approach to designing. Systems design doesn't discount user goals and needs—they can be used to set the goal of the system. But in this approach, users are de-emphasized in favor of *context*. Designers using system design focus on the whole context of use, not just individual objects or devices. Systems design can be thought of as a rigorous look at the broad context in which a product or service will be used.

Systems design outlines the components that systems should have: a goal, a sensor, a comparator, and an actuator. The job of the designer, then, becomes that of designing those components. In this way, systems design removes the guesswork and fuzziness of the other approaches and provides a clear roadmap for designers to follow.

Let's use the classic example of a heating system to illustrate the main parts of any system (**Figure 2.2**):

Figure 2.2

A system, based on a diagram by Hugh Dubberly and Paul Pangaro, 2003.

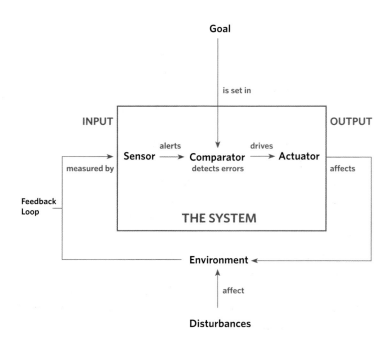

▶ **Goal.** This is not the users' goal, but rather the goal of the system as a whole, which can be drawn from user goals. The goal states the ideal relationship between the system and the environment it lives in. In a heating system, an example of a goal may be keeping your house at 72 degrees Fahrenheit.

▶ **Environment.** Where does the system "live"? Is it digital or analog or both? The environment in the heating system example is the house itself.

▶ **Sensors.** How does the system detect changes in the environment? A heating system has a thermostat with a thermometer (**Figure 2.3**) to detect temperature changes.

▶ **Disturbances.** Changes are called disturbances; these are elements in the environment that change the environment in both expected and unexpected ways. In the heating system example, a disturbance is a drop or rise in temperature.

▶ **Comparator.** The comparator embodies the goal within the system. It compares the current state (the environment) to the desired state (the goal). Any difference between the two is seen by the system as an error, which the system seeks to correct. In the heating system example, the comparator can be a tiny computer or a mercury switch that compares what the sensor tells it about the environment (for example, "72 degrees...72 degrees...72 degrees...71 degrees...71 degrees") to the goal ("Keep the house at 72 degrees").

COURTESY ISTOCKPHOTO

Figure 2.3

A thermostat contains the sensor, comparator, actuator, and controls of a heating system.

▶ **Actuator.** If the comparator says, ah, something is different (an "error") by examining the data coming from the sensor, it sends a command to the actuator (in this case, the boiler). Actuators are a means of making changes (output) to the environment. In this case, the actuator makes heat.

▶ **Feedback.** With output comes feedback. Feedback is a message about whether or not a goal was achieved or maintained—whether or not an error was detected. In this example, feedback would report either that the house is still at 71 degrees or that is now at 72 degrees and the heater can be turned off.

▸   **Controls.** Controls are means of manually manipulating the parts of the system (except the environment). In this example, you use a control to set the temperature you want the house to be. Another control might trigger the actuator and turn the heat on.

There are two types of disturbances to the environment that might affect our heating system. The first consists of expected disturbances, such as the temperature dropping. The second type consists of unexpected disturbances—things that would fall outside of the expected range of input. These types of disturbances typically cause the system to crash or behave in odd ways. In our heating example, such an event might be a sudden 100-degree drop in temperature.

To make most unexpected disturbances expected (and thus make the system more stable), systems need what's called **requisite variety**. The system needs an assortment of responses to deal with a range of situations. These responses can be anything from error messages ("You are being sent 1 million e-mail messages!") to workarounds ("You are being sent 1 million e-mail messages. Should I delete them or deliver them in chunks of 10,000?") to mechanisms to prevent the system from failing (deleting all incoming e-mails over a certain number). Systems without requisite variety crash often, which may be fine for a prototype, but not so great for, say, an air-traffic control system.

Feedback is output from the system that reports that something has just happened: input was received from the environment, the comparator was changed, and so on. You get feedback from your computer almost every time you press a key. We'll discuss feedback for users more in Chapter 7, but we'll simply note here that systems without feedback either will not work or will be bewildering.

Systems design isn't only about digital products, of course. Most services, for example, are systems consisting of digital and analog components. Your local coffee shop is filled with sensors, comparators, and actuators, only you probably know them as the shop employees. However, the objections and distaste many designers have about systems design spring from examples just such as these. Many designers feel that systems design is dehumanizing, turning people into robotic components in a very synthetic arrangement. And indeed, systems design is a very logical, analytical approach to interaction design. Emotions, passion, and whim have very little place in this sort of design, except as disturbances in the environment that need to be countered. Someone screaming angrily in the coffee shop is a major disturbance!

The greatest strength of systems design, however, is that it is useful for seeing the big picture—for its holistic view of a project. No product exists in a vacuum, after all, and systems design forces designers to take into account the environment that the product or service inhabits. By focusing on the broad context of use and the interplay of the components, designers gain a better understanding of the circumstances surrounding a product or service.

Hugh Dubberly on Systems Design

Hugh Dubberly is founder and principal at Dubberly Design Office (DDO), an interaction design consultancy in San Francisco. Before forming DDO, he served as vice president for design at AOL/Netscape and as creative director at Apple Computer, Inc. He has also taught at San Jose State University and Stanford University.

What is systems design?

Systems design is simply the design of systems. It implies a systematic and rigorous approach to design—an approach demanded by the scale and complexity of many systems problems.

Where did systems design come from?

Systems design first appeared shortly before World War II as engineers grappled with complex communications and control problems. They formalized their work in the new disciplines of information theory, operations research, and cybernetics. In the 1960s, members of the design methods movement (especially Horst Rittel and others at Ulm and Berkeley) transferred this knowledge to the design world. Systems design continues to flourish at schools interested in design planning and within the world of computer science. Among its most important legacies is a research field known as design rationale, which concerns systems for making and documenting design decisions.

What can designers learn from systems design?

Today, ideas from design methods and systems design may be more relevant to designers than ever before—as more and more designers collaborate on designing software and complex information spaces. Frameworks suggested by systems design are especially useful in modeling interaction and conversation. They are also useful in modeling the design process itself.

What is the most important thing to be aware of in systems design?

A systems approach to design asks:

- ▶   For this situation, what is the system?
- ▶   What is the environment?
- ▶   What goal does the system have in relation to its environment?
- ▶   What is the feedback loop by which the system corrects its actions?
- ▶   How does the system measure whether it has achieved its goal?
- ▶   Who defines the system, environment, goal, etc.—and monitors it?
- ▶   What resources does the system have for maintaining the relationship it desires?
- ▶   Are its resources sufficient to meet its purpose?

Is systems design incompatible with user-centered design?

A systems approach to design is entirely compatible with a user-centered approach. Indeed, the core of both approaches is understanding user goals. A systems approach looks at users in relation to a context and in terms of their interaction with devices, with each other, and with themselves.

What is the relationship between systems design and cybernetics?

Cybernetics (the science of feedback) provides an approach to systems and a set of frameworks and tools. Among the most important ideas for designers:

- ▶   Definition of a system depends on point of view (subjectivity).
- ▶   We are responsible for our actions (ethical stance).
- ▶   All interaction is a form of conversation.
- ▶   All conversation involves goals, understandings, and agreements.

Are there times when systems design isn't appropriate?

A systems approach to design is most appropriate for projects involving large systems or systems of systems. Such projects typically involve many people, from many disciplines, working together over an extended period of time. They need tools to cope with their project's complexity: to define goals, facilitate communications, and manage processes. Solo designers working on small projects may find the same tools a bit cumbersome for their needs.

Genius Design

The fourth major design approach is something I named **genius design**. Genius design relies almost solely on the wisdom and experience of the designer to make design decisions. Designers use their best judgment as to what users want and then design the product based on that judgment. User involvement, if it occurs at all, comes at the end of the process, when users test what the designers have made to make sure it really works as the designer has predicted.

Compared to the rigor of the other three approaches, genius design seems almost cavalier. Yet this is how most interaction design is done today, either by choice—Apple, supposedly for privacy reasons, does very little user research or testing at all—or by necessity. Many designers work in organizations that don't provide funding or time for research, so the designers are left to their own devices.

This is not to say that designers who practice genius design don't consider users—they do. It's simply that the designers either don't have the resources or the inclination to involve users in the design process. Designers use their personal knowledge (and frequently the knowledge of the organization they're working for and research from others) to determine users' wants, needs, and expectations.

Genius design can create some impressive designs, such as Apple's iPod (**Figure 2.4**).

It can also create some impressive failures, such as Apple's first hand-held device, the Newton, which was too bulky and difficult to use for most users. Aside from market forces (not an inconsiderable factor), the success of genius-designed products rests heavily on the skill of the designer. Thus, genius design is probably best practiced by experienced designers, who have encountered many different types of problems and can draw upon solutions from many past projects.

COURTESY APPLE

Figure 2.4

Apple's iPod was created using genius design by designers such as Jonathan Ive.

It probably also works best when the designer is one of the potential users, although this can be a serious trap as well. The designers who created the Windows 95 operating system probably considered themselves the users, but while they understood perfectly well how the OS worked, ordinary users suffered. Because of their intimate understanding of how the product or service they designed was created and their inside knowledge of the decisions behind it, the designers will know much more about the functionality of the product or service than will most end users.

Unfortunately, while genius design is best practiced by experienced designers, it's often attempted by inexperienced designers. Many designers use this approach because it is, frankly, easier than the other three. It requires a lot less effort to noodle on a whiteboard than it does to research users or artfully assemble the components of a system. Designers, especially new designers, should practice genius design with care, for instincts can be dead wrong.

Genius design has many strengths, however, especially for an experienced designer. It's a fast and personal way to work, and the final design, perhaps more than with the other approaches, reflects the designer's own sensibilities. It is also the most flexible approach, allowing designers to focus their efforts where they see fit. By following their own muses, designers may be able to think more broadly and innovate more freely.

Jim Leftwich on Rapid Expert Design

James Leftwich, IDSA, is Chief Experience Officer at SeeqPod, and founder of Orbit Interaction, a pioneering interaction design consultancy located in Palo Alto, California. He has over 25 years of broad consulting and professional experience in the area of Human Interface development and related intellectual property strategies.

You don't like the term "genius design" very much. How come?

I find it difficult to believe that [with that name] it's an approach that many people would aspire to. Young designers may simply think, "Well, hey, I'm not a genius, so I guess this approach isn't for me." Second, designers of any type are likely to cringe at the term, and would rather die before announcing to the world that they practice "genius design."

Jim Leftwich on Rapid Expert Design *(continued)*

I refer to it as Rapid Expert Design, rather than "genius" (even if some talent and inherent capabilities may be a definite plus just like in sports).

Given that I believe Rapid Expert Design is a valid and largely missing and under-examined approach to interactive product development (as well as re-development, improvement, turnarounds, etc.), I think it's important how the "framing" is carried out. I'm certain you're familiar with the concept of framing [see Chapter 3], and the importance it plays in all forms of communication and debate. It's very similar to how political issues are framed, and how when one partisan side (or anyone, for that matter) defines an issue in a particular way, it affects all the subsequent discussion and perception.

That's why I find the term you used very unhelpful in propagating an incredibly needed and valid approach.

Why is this approach so important?

We're slogging through a world with a nearly uncountable number of undesigned and unad-dressed user interface and functional problems and inadequacies. Long, drawn-out, and process-oriented approaches to the development of interactive products and services have left us with precious few clear wins. Very few interactive products and designs stem from sin-gular or whole visions and architectural guidance. They are, instead, the result of groupthink, rearview mirror timid incrementalism, bureaucratic and disempowered designer-watering-down, and a whole host of other threats and obstacles.

How can we teach designers to practice Rapid Expert Design?

This is where the catch is, and why it's so important to start with an acknowledgement of the validity of the approach and realization of how Rapid Expert Designers are trained and exercised. The only way to become proficient at the R.E.D. approach is through apprentic-ing and incrementally using the approach on projects of increasing scale and complexity. A young designer that ambitiously bites off an entire consumer product may indeed fail. However, it's important that they begin learning (along with more experienced designers) how to approach things in this manner, in smaller steps, so that they can eventually become more proficient at R.E.D.

Summary

Most designers feel more comfortable with one design approach than the others, although most designers mix approaches as they work. A designer's temperament, personal philosophy, and view of work and of a project's users will help determine which approach the designer prefers. But the best designers are those who can move between these different approaches as the situation warrants, so it's good to know them all.

For Further Reading

About Face 3: The Essentials of Interaction Design, Alan Cooper, Robert Reimann, and David Cronin

Designing for People, Henry Dreyfuss

Cybernetics, Second Edition: or the Control and Communication in the Animal and the Machine, Norbert Wiener

General System Theory: Foundations, Development, Applications, Ludwig Von Bertalanffy

Activity-Centered Design: An Ecological Approach to Designing Smart Tools and Usable Systems, Geri Gay and Helene Hembrooke

Acting with Technology: Activity Theory and Interaction Design, Victor Kaptelinin and Bonnie Nardi

3

Design Strategy

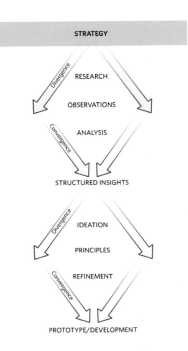

Designing a product for everyone, everywhere, for all time is not realistic. Before you design anything, you need to determine what should be designed, and why. Just as importantly, you need to determine what is *not* going to be designed. You have to understand what the value of the proposed product is: both for users and for the sponsoring organization. And you have to figure out how this product will fit in—or, better yet, redefine—its product category, and how it will differentiate itself from other products on the market.

This is the essence of design strategy.

What Is Design Strategy?

At the beginning of a project, instead of saying, "Let's design this new widget," the first questions that should be asked are, "What should we be designing that will meet our organization's needs and the needs of our customers?" and "How should that solution be manifest: as a widget or something else entirely?" This is what design strategy work helps determine.

NOTE *Of course, for smaller projects, and especially those on existing projects, such as designing a wizard or adding a piece of functionality, a deep dive into strategy could be a waste of time. Strategy's best application is for new products or existing products that are getting a complete redesign.*

Design strategy is the product and project planning that takes place at the beginning of the design process. It is a combination of defining a vision for the end state of a project, and determining the tactics needed to execute on that vision. Design strategy is composed of several parts:

▸   Framing the problem or opportunity to be addressed

▸   Determining key differentiators for the product to be designed

▸   Visualizing and selling the strategy to the organization

▸   Creating a product roadmap and a project plan to achieve the goals of the project

Design strategy (along with design research, covered in Chapter 4) helps organizations determine what products to create over the short- and long-term, and it should be the first step in any design process. To begin a project without knowing what is being built and why is a recipe for serious difficulties deeper into the project. Strategy provides a framework for designers to justify the project to the business: why resources should be spent to design, produce, and market this product.

While many organizations still engage designers only after the strategy has been determined, it behooves designers to understand that strategy before beginning design work.

Strategy as a way of thinking has its roots in a 1980 book by Harvard Business School professor Michael Porter entitled *Competitive Strategy: Techniques for Analyzing Industries and Competitors*. Porter said that design strategy doesn't mean **operational effectiveness**—being able to do what your competitor does more effectively—because eventually, this stops working. There is only so much efficiency you can get out of a system, and your competitors eventually figure out how to make their own operations as effective as yours. Instead, Porter says, strategy is about being different from your competitors: either performing different activities, or else performing similar activities differently. The purpose of strategy is to determine what *not* to do so that you prioritize ideas and can focus on setting your product apart.

> NOTE *One alternate view of strategy, which is seemingly practiced at organizations like Sony, Google, and Samsung, is to simply execute on core competencies such as engineering, moving into different markets as they become known or popular without much regard for differentiation.*

Carving out a unique place in the market and tuning the organization (and the products it produces) to deliver products and services that fit that position gives a company a clear **competitive advantage** that is hard to replicate, and thus valuable.

Design Strategy and Business Strategy

A design strategy that doesn't work for the overall organization's strategy is like a bad organ transplant: the host body will reject it. Any design strategy for a product (the **product strategy**) has to work with the organization's overall strategy to be successful.

NOTE   *This is not to say that a good design strategy (and the resulting product) cannot change the overall strategy of a company: it certainly can. After the iPod, "Apple Computer" became simply "Apple" as it realized its future was also in consumer electronics.*

When people speak of "strategy" within organizations, they can be talking about any one of these three things:

▶ **Corporate strategy.** Deals with how the organization is run: company structure, finances, and human resources. Corporate strategy also oversees how the other two strategy types are put into effect.

▶ **Operational strategy.** Looks at efficiency and effectiveness in processes. IT and (obviously) operations are in this category.

▶ **Business strategy.** Deals with generating new products and looking for new markets. Marketing, business analysis, and design are typically here.

Depending on the type of product being proposed, the product (and thus the strategy) could affect one or more of these. A new product may require different personnel, new IT infrastructure, and new marketing, for example. But product strategy almost always affects the last category. Thus, it behooves designers to have some knowledge of an organization's business strategy to make sure whatever will be designed fits into the big picture. A project that doesn't work with the business strategy will likely fail or at least not succeed as strongly as it could have, because they will be fighting the organization internally throughout their lifecycle.

Porter also defined the three types of generic business strategies. It's important to know which one the organization you are working for is pursuing, because it will affect the design decisions throughout the project:

▶ **Cost leadership strategy.** This strategy is all about making use of economies of scale to efficiently create basic, no-frills products that can be made at a low cost and widely sold. Dell and Southwest Airlines are examples of companies that mostly follow a cost leadership strategy.

▶ **Focus strategy.** This strategy is about effectively targeting niches, creating specialized products for a select few target markets. Medical device manufacturers and companies such as Leapfrog pursue a focus strategy.

▶ **Differentiation strategy.** This strategy is about creating products that are seen as unique and therefore a premium price can be attached to them. Apple and Bang & Olufsen are examples of companies that follow a differentiation strategy.

In the simplest terms, designers should understand how the organizations they work for make money, and how the organizations plan to increase their revenues in the future. Ultimately, this is the context in which design work is judged, at least internally. (Users have their own criteria, which we'll discuss in Chapters 4 and 8.)

Learning this overall business strategy is part of framing the problem to be addressed.

Brandon Schauer on Design Strategy

Brandon Schauer is an experience design director at San Francisco design firm Adaptive Path, where he speaks, writes, trains, and practices experience design as a differentiator for business strategy. Brandon holds a Master of Design from the Institute of Design and a MBA from the Stuart School of Business. Brandon is also a co-author of Subject to Change: Creating Great Products & Services for an Uncertain World.

Why should interaction designers care about business strategy?

The projects an interaction designer works on are determined by the business strategy. The ideas and designs generated by an interaction designer are supported and funded if they fit the business strategy.

Many designers now research and plan for the larger context of people's lives when creating interactions. Well, there's also the context of the business strategy that is just as critical to the success of their work; it too should be researched and planned for.

What do you see as the relationship between design strategy and business strategy?

General business strategy should inform what activities a business engages in and how it goes about those activities. IKEA invests time and money in creating explanatory catalogs, signage, and other store displays. That's an activity they engage in so they don't have to provide more expensive customer service. It's a strategic tradeoff IKEA makes in their business strategy.

A good design strategy should connect the practice of design within an organization to that overall business strategy. When you look at the design of IKEA furniture, you see that it can be flat-packed in boxes, self-assembled by customers with minimal tools and instructions, and can be manufactured in mass quantities for a low cost. All of these furniture design decisions by the in-house design staff reinforce IKEA's overall strategy to provide low cost furniture for a broad market. Design strategy infuses the business strategy into the everyday design decisions.

What is the most crucial part of doing design strategy and why?

Focus, vision, customer value, and scope are all key elements of a good design strategy, but I believe the most crucial is your ability to communicate and enact your strategy. Otherwise, it's all just a bunch of hand-waving.

Luckily designers have strong visual communication skills to show what their strategy delivers to the business and the customer—this quarter, next quarter, and next year. However, designers need to work much harder at verbally explaining the value of that design strategy in terms that the rest of the organization understands.

Take the example of Sam Lucente, the VP of Design at HP. When CEO Mark Hurd was focused on operational efficiencies, Lucente didn't pitch the standardization of HP logos across all products as an improvement to the presence of the HP brand. Instead, he estimated that shipping products with a standard logo would save HP $50 million of development and manufacturing costs. That got the CEO's attention.

What's the biggest mistake designers make when doing strategic work?

Designers assume that because they can't create a complex financial model that they shouldn't bother interacting with numbers at all. Wrong. It takes very little effort to find out what metrics a business runs on, and slightly more effort to figure out how your work affects those numbers. An estimate of the value of a new interaction is simply just another kind of a prototype to be created.

You've said designers should strive for "The Long Wow." What is that?

The Long Wow is a means to achieving long-term customer loyalty through systematically impressing your customers again and again. For most businesses, customer loyalty has become essential, yet these same businesses create artificial loyalty programs based on ID cards and memberships rather than delivering the great products and services that customers want in the first place.

I started using Google Maps because of the ease of dragging the map. But Google Maps didn't require me to sign-up or join as a member. I've kept using it because it's steadily impressed me with great new uses, from direction for mass transit to street views and traffic information.

Interaction designers can achieve a Long Wow by not just thinking about the current project, but demonstrating how the current project can be a platform for delivering the next "wow" moment for the customer. Such additional planning and foresight is the basis for a design strategy focused on great customer experiences.

Framing the Problem

There's an old joke among software developers. When something works in an unexpected but strangely effective way, the developers often kid, "Oh, that's not a bug. That's a feature." While this is usually only a joke, designers can use the same technique of reframing the problem when tackling their own projects. In fact, there's an old joke among designers: "It's not a problem. It's an opportunity."

Typically, before a designer gets involved in a project, a business encounters or discovers a problem or a perceived problem. A current product isn't selling or working well or is simply out of style—witness the launch of new mobile phones every six months. Or a competitor has launched a better product, as occurred in the mid 1990s as companies intensely vied to produce the best Internet browser. Or a new market has opened up and products need to be created for that market, which is what happened with Facebook widgets and iPhone applications. These "problems" become the basis for involving a designer.

The problem with problems, especially the problems that interaction designers tend to get involved with, is that they are often messy and ill-defined. Unless the problem is simple and narrow (like, say, users can't find the Submit button at the end of a form), don't take any problem that you are given—or even one you've defined yourself—at face value. What seems at first glance to be simple often really isn't—and the reverse is rarely true.

Consider the simple problem of an online form on which users seem to have trouble finding the Submit button at the form's end. The simple solution might be just to move the button to a better place or make the button more prominent through color, size, or shape. But this issue could also be an indicator of a larger problem. Maybe the form is too long. Maybe users don't understand why they are filling out the form, and the problem isn't that they can't find the button, but that they abandon the form in the middle, not caring to finish it. Or maybe they are afraid to click the button because they don't know what will happen next. And so on. Simple problems can be indicators of larger ones.

> NOTE *That being said, while working, interaction designers shouldn't overly complicate things and should pick their battles. Sometimes a button problem is just a button problem. Not every project needs to be completely rethought and broken down. The teams that interaction designers work with would hate them if they constantly did that. But— and this will be a theme in this book—be deliberate in the choices you make. If making the button bigger will solve most of the problem, well then, make the button bigger.*

Indeed, the kinds of problems interaction designers are often involved in are those called **wicked problems**, a term coined in the 1973 by design theorist Horst Rittel.[1] Wicked problems are situations that aren't fully understood and have fuzzy boundaries. They have lots of affected people (stakeholders) with a say in them; they have lots of constraints, and they have no clear solution.

In order to attempt a design solution to the problem, designers, along with client stakeholders, first need to frame the problem. There needs to be some sort of border around the project—a shared understanding of the issues involved—so that the problem can be worked on. One of the worst things a

---

1 See for instance "Dilemmas in a General Theory of Planning," Horst Rittel, Horst and Melvin Webber in Policy Sciences, Vol. 4

designer can do is solve the wrong problem. Designers can't just solve problems; they also have to **problem set**.

Problem setting is when designers, in the words of Donald Schön from *The Reflective Practitioner*, "name the things to which we will attend and frame the context in which we will attend to them." Problems and the projects that are created to deal with them aren't usually a given; they are human constructs around a messy situation. Thus, the first part of any design strategy work is to frame the situation, to put design into the problem and impose some sort of order onto it. By "framing and naming," designers want to both understand the situation and, eventually, to change it. When framing, designers have no idea what the implications of the new frame will be, just that within the frame, they have created a space in which they can use the design process to try to solve the problem.

For example, let's say a company's new mobile device isn't selling well. There could be any number of reasons for this: everything from global economic issues to surly salespeople. In order for the design process to really get started, designers have to figure out where the problem actually is, frame it, and then apply their talents there—or not.

Framing the problem means doing two things: zooming out to establish a border around the problem, then zooming back in to determine the details of the parts. In many ways, this is a microcosm of the design process as a whole: use divergent thinking to explore possibilities and opportunities, then converge on tangible artifacts to define and refine a solution.

A strategic framework for a problem could be any number of things: a metaphor for the problem space; a story that encompasses the various aspects of the problem; a creative brief that describes what is in and what's out of the project; a visualization; a product plan. It's anything that helps communicate to the organization and the design team where the borders of the problem are and what the purpose of the project is.

The first step of this process is to gather information. Designers need input and other points of view from clients, stakeholders, colleagues, teammates, and others who have maybe thought about this situation (or similar situations). Designers typically get this information from three places: traditional research, the design brief, and stakeholder interviews. (Designers can, of course, get input from users, too; see Chapter 4.)

Traditional Research

The best strategies start with a candid assessment of the organization, its resources, its customers, brand, and position in the market. Traditional research is a good place to begin this, and should be done before other kinds of strategic activities (such as stakeholder interviews).

It's almost silly to say, but a simple Internet search on the subject you are dealing with and the company you are working for can be extremely revealing, as is examining company reports, press releases, and documentation, as well as books, newspapers, and magazines. These are the sources of traditional research.

Unless specifically told not to, designers should feel free to consult outside sources as part of the information-gathering process. Thanks to a little thing called the Internet, we now have access to information quickly and easily from many different sources. Designers should make good use of it! Very few projects are in an area that no one has thought about before. Even a cursory search of the Internet, and especially of e-mail list archives, discussion boards, and technical and academic journals, will likely turn up information about the subject area, as well as information about the company, its market, and its competitors.

> NOTE *Traditional research does not include patent research. Interaction designers are encouraged to avoid patent filings and articles about patents at all costs. The penalties for patent infringement are high, and will be higher (at least in the U.S.) if the designers knew about the patent beforehand. Let the lawyers handle patents. Ironically, not knowing about a patent is the best defense for patent infringement cases.*

As any doctoral candidate can attest, a person can spend a nearly infinite amount of time gathering information. It's important to focus this part of the process on gathering *germane* information that will eventually find its way into the solution. The goal is to gain general knowledge about the project's subject area (and perhaps related areas), and also deep knowledge about the particular problem that is being addressed.

Design Brief

The design brief is a document, usually from the client (or an internal business manager or unit hereafter referred to as a client), although increasingly it is being made by the design team. The design brief should lay out the reasons for employing the designer (the problem) and often make suggestions for the solution as well. The brief is an excellent starting point for gathering information. Briefs can contain such information as brand considerations, technical constraints, expected timetable and deliverables, detailed goals of the project, and contact information for major stakeholders.

Design briefs are becoming less and less common, so they can also be a deliverable that the designer generates as a result of the stakeholder interviews, traditional research, and competitive analysis. The brief then becomes a way of capturing and communicating what was learned during the initial information-gathering period of the project.

In a client-supplied brief, designers usually get some insight into what the client thinks will make a successful project. This likely won't be spelled out; it may just be a throwaway line like "We want to make the new application fresh" embedded within a 50-page document filled with complicated business and technical goals. But if the designer meets all those goals but creates a conservative design that doesn't address the client's desire for "freshness," the client will be unhappy.

The brief should be only a starting point in discussions about the project. Indeed, the brief could raise as many questions as it solves. What exactly does making the application "fresh" mean? That's where stakeholder interviews come in.

Stakeholder Interviews

Stakeholders are people who have a particular interest in, and/or influence on, the outcome of the project.

Stakeholder interviews (**Figure 3.1**) are usually one of the designer's first tasks on any project. The interviews are the client's chance to tell the designer why the client thinks that the project is needed, to reveal the client's frame around the project. As stated earlier in this chapter, these reasons may be mistaken, and the designer should feel free to challenge them. The problem may not be what the client thinks it is, and the designer will have to do her own problem setting.

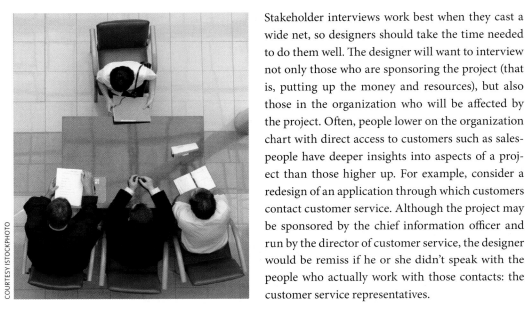

COURTESY ISTOCKPHOTO

Stakeholder interviews work best when they cast a wide net, so designers should take the time needed to do them well. The designer will want to interview not only those who are sponsoring the project (that is, putting up the money and resources), but also those in the organization who will be affected by the project. Often, people lower on the organization chart with direct access to customers such as salespeople have deeper insights into aspects of a project than those higher up. For example, consider a redesign of an application through which customers contact customer service. Although the project may be sponsored by the chief information officer and run by the director of customer service, the designer would be remiss if he or she didn't speak with the people who actually work with those contacts: the customer service representatives.

Figure 3.1

If possible, conduct stakeholder interviews in-person and individually. Try to meet with as many influential and powerful people as you can.

Interaction designers should not only ask the How and What questions, but also the Why questions. Why does this work this way? Why is it important to sell a million ball bearings a month? Why should this application be on a mobile phone? Why questions help designers avoid questions that don't provide much information, such as those that can be answered with a yes or no.

Here are some sample questions that could be asked in most stakeholder interviews:

▶   Who are you and what is your role in this organization?

▶   Why is this project important to you? To the organization?

▶   What would make a successful project?

▶   Has anyone ever tried to address this problem before?

▶   What doesn't this project cover?

▶   If we could only do one thing with this project, what would that be?

▶   How could this project affect your day-to-day life?

▶   Are there any issues about this project I should be aware of?

▶   What are the risks in doing this project? What could make it fail?

▶   What are your competitors doing in this space?

▶   Who else should I talk to about this project?

Stakeholder interviews are the time for the client to tell the designer (or for the designer to probe about) the business goals of the project. Business goals can be anything from hard numbers ("We need to sell 5 million ball bearings a day") to acquiring new customers or entering new markets to soft, company-brand goals ("We need a more elegant interface"). But again, the designer needs to be careful! Look for the *unstated* goals of the project. Sometimes, organizations want to use projects for different ends, such as to merge two departments or add staff, and will use the design project as a means to do so. Solutions that run contrary to these unstated goals could be greeted coldly.

Stakeholder interviews also help designers understand the *constraints* of the project. No project is without some boundaries that for business, technical, or resource reasons cannot be crossed—at least not crossed easily. Constraints can be placed on a number of entities, such as marketing, accounting, management, IT, and of course, users. Sometimes constraints are as simple as the medium in which the project will be created ("We want a Web site" or "We'd like to make a new mobile device"). Sometimes constraints are a lot more complex ("We've already sold advertising for each Web page, so you need to design space for that" or "This robot can make only left turns right now and occasionally explodes"). Interaction designers need to capture and document constraints throughout the course of the project, in everything from stakeholder interview notes to wireframes. These constraints will shape the design decisions that are made later in the process (see Chapter 7).

Metrics and Return on Investment (ROI)

By learning about the business goals of the project, the designer should also learn about the overall business strategy as well as what the organization will consider a successful project at the end ("We sold 10 million ball bearings today!"). These measures are referred to as **success metrics**. Success metrics let you take an objective look at a project's result to see what progress has been made toward its goal. Success metrics for the project should ideally be tied to the overall success metrics of the organization as a whole (increased market share, higher profits, and so on).

In short, get some basic numbers that can be used as a baseline to compare against once the project is over.

Designers have a selfish reason to find out the impact of their work on the organization. Demonstrating value—particularly monetary value via affecting the bottom line—to an organization proves that design isn't what is known as a **cost center**. Cost centers such as human resources or research and development only add value to the company indirectly, and these are often the parts of the organization that are viewed as the least valuable and most easily disbanded or downsized when times get tough.

Evaluating success, of course, is much easier for projects that have hard-numbers expectations than for those with softer goals. It's sometimes not easy to measure what businesses call return on investment (ROI) for inter-action design. If an organization expects a design to meet an ROI goal, the designer needs to be sure some mechanism for measuring success is in place *before* the design work begins. Designers should want some sort of baseline criteria culled from the existing situation that they can then use to mea-sure the new design against. For example, before beginning the redesign of a Web site registration process, the designer should get some quantitative data: numbers, in other words. It takes six minutes to register. On an ease-of-use scale of 1 to 5, with 5 being excellent, users currently rate registration as a 2. According to server logs, half the people stop registering after the second page. With this baseline data in hand, at the end of the project, the designer can measure the new solution and compare the new data to the old and also to the goals of the project. If the designer has done the job well, the numbers will likely show it.

Competitive Analysis

In order to be taken seriously, interaction designers have to understand what the current landscape of competitors is. It is important to understand **market factors**: overall trends in the market, what industry leaders are doing, what products are popular and/or selling well (and why), and the latest technology. This is definitely not to say that designers should slavishly follow the market or trends, but rather that they should know about what is currently available so that they don't inadvertently replicate what is already out there, and thus create little or no value for the organization they are working for.

The other reason to do competitive analysis is simple: to find holes in the market and unsolved problems that a new product could address and pro-vide competitive advantage.

When doing competitive analysis, always look for untraditional competitors as well as the ones that directly compete for market share. For example, traditionally the competitors of news organizations were other news organizations. Now they compete with blogs, photo-sharing Web sites, and news aggregators as well. A useful tool to find these competitors is to ask, "What would customers do if all the traditional competitors went away? What would they do instead?"

Once you have your list of competitors (and stakeholder interviews may turn up more), the next task is to figure out the criteria by which you will be comparing and contrasting them. These can be broad (brand, tone, users) or detailed (analysis/presence of a particular feature).

The data you collect when doing a competitive analysis (**Table 3.1**) can be anything from a simple yes/no ("Does Product X have search?"); multiple choice ("Type of search: Site only"); a scale ("How well does search work on a scale of 1 to 10?"); or a description ("Search returns 10 results per screen").

Table 3.1 Sample Competitive Analysis

Competitor	Touchscreen?	Years on Market	Brand Promise	Customers
Competitor 1	No	7	Ease-of-use, simplicity	Beginners
Competitor 2	Yes	1	Powerful, robust	Professionals
Competitor 3	No	2	Sophisticated	Professionals

Aside from this more raw, at-a-glance view of the data, overviews and conclusions drawn from a competitive analysis can be a compelling means of showing market opportunities (**Figure 3.2**) and promoting the project internally (see "Visualization and Visioning" later in the chapter).

By the end of the framing process, you should know a few things: the boundaries and scope of the project; what the internal context of the project is (that is, why the business wants to do the project); the external context (the marketplace and competitors); and

Figure 3.2

In this two-by-two, different pet-related Web sites are plotted on a simple graph. The axes of the graph represent the scope of the content (commercial versus advice/information) and specialization (number of pet types supported).

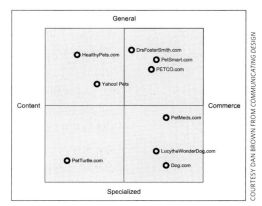

COURTESY DAN BROWN FROM COMMUNICATING DESIGN

some important metrics around the project. Now it is time to determine how you can position the product into this environment and make it successful for the organization and valuable (that is, worth paying for) for its users.

Determining Differentiators

A major step in the design strategy process is determining what the **value proposition** is. The value proposition is what customers will get in return for buying or using this product over another, similar product. If you are not adding value for a user, you are simply making the product different for the sake of being different, and this is not good design.

Donald Reinertsen in *Managing the Design Factory* challenges designers to define the value proposition in 25 words or less. "Most successful products have a clear and simple value proposition. Buyers typically make their choice between competing products on the basis of three or four factors," Reinertsen says.

Traditionally, value propositions have focused on two things: cost and quality. Either a product is cheaper than its competitor (its **price point** is lower), or else it is better quality. (This can be a false dichotomy, and designers should almost always focus on the highest possible quality at the lowest possible cost—or at least the lowest possible cost to **manufacture**.)

Increasingly, design has become part of the quality equation, especially around how devices work. A 2006 study by Elke den Ouden found that most electronic products that were returned to the store weren't broken, but instead worked exactly as designed; they were returned because customers expected them to do more than they did or they just didn't like the design, or they simply couldn't figure them out.[2] Interaction designers can provide business and customer value simply by making products work better (and thus decreasing returns and/or abandonment).

But even more than that, the overall experience of using the product has become a major differentiator, and interaction design has a significant part to play in that. A **differentiator**—something that sets a product apart from its competitors—has too frequently been features. "Our Web site is not just another social

---

2 See an analysis of her findings at "Soft Reliability: a 'New' Angle on Quality Management (or Usability?)" at www.uselog.com/2008/01/soft-reliability-angle-on-quality.html

network; we also have e-mail." But features, unless protected by patents (and even then), are eventually replicated. And while features are certainly important, designers should strive to find long-term differentiation. This is a much harder proposition, and designers should look for those opportunities throughout the design process, particularly around areas of behavior.

Interaction designers can create differentiators both in how the product behaves (see Chapters 7 and 8), and also in the behaviors it engenders (**Figure 3.3**). Let's look at video cameras, for example. Most video cameras focused on the behavior of shooting the video. Flip Video, instead of competing against Sony, Canon, JVC, and so on, focused on the behavior of transferring video off the camera onto a computer, and thus gained a competitive advantage.

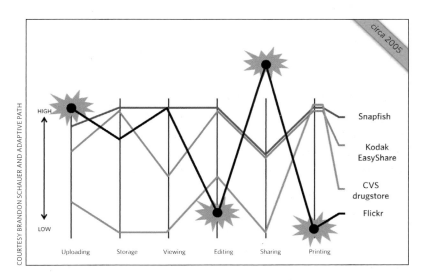

Figure 3.3

A chart comparing the differentiation of photography Web site Flickr (circa 2005) with its then-rivals. Inspired by *Blue Ocean Strategy* by W. Chan Kim and Renée Mauborgne.

Aside from product behavior, there are some known ways of differentiating your product:

▶ **Specialization.** Target your product to a very specialized market that is currently underserved. Kayak.com differentiates from Google simply by focusing on one area (travel).

▸   **Generalize.** The opposite of specialization is to broaden the market by taking what would otherwise be a specialized product and designing it for a wider audience. A classic example of this is rolling luggage, which was originally designed for flight crews.

▸   **Localize or change context.** A product that works well in one context could be redesigned to work well in another context. Touchscreen kiosks were in use at point-of-sale locations for years before airlines started to use them for passenger check-in.

Any differentiators should be checked against the value proposition. Otherwise, you are just making the product different to be different, and that isn't typically a good design practice. A differentiator that doesn't support the reasons the customer would buy or use the product will just lead to a confused or, at best, a shallowly-differentiated product. For example, most people enjoy music, but every product doesn't need a music player incorporated into it. Features added without an understanding of the real value proposition don't add value; in fact, they do the opposite by confusing the purpose of the product, which often translates into an overly-confusing interface and form.

Two exercises, which can be done alone or as a group, that have proved helpful in determining the value proposition and key differentiators are the **elevator pitch** and the **advertisement**. The elevator pitch just formalizes Reinertsen's challenge of "25 words or less" into an exercise to do just that. Describe what you want to design so that you can explain what it is, what makes it unique, and why someone would use it instead of something else. It should be able to be spoken in less than 30 seconds and understandable to someone who isn't involved in the project. Similarly, the advertisement exercise is one where the packaging and advertising for the finished product are imagined and created. The ads can be anything from online banner ads to printed pieces to mock TV commercials. Both of these exercises are not only helpful in defining the value proposition and differentiators, but they can also be useful tools for helping sell the project internally.

Fighting Feature-itis

People love features. We enjoy comparing products side-by-side and choosing the one with the most features. We figure, logically, that more features for the same money is a better value. Companies love features, too. It gives them something to easily market and talk about. It also allows them to simply replicate what their competitors are doing without having to come up with real differentiators. But features, as noted before, are a poor long-term strategy because they are eventually replicated. And more features does not necessarily make a better product; in fact, it can make for a less usable, more confused one that, instead of doing one thing well, does many things poorly.

An article by James Surowiecki[3] points out the feature paradox: "Although consumers find overloaded gadgets unmanageable, they also find them attractive. It turns out that when we look at a new product in a store we tend to think that the more features there are, the better. It's only once we get the product home and try to use it that we realize the virtues of simplicity."

Don Norman's advice[4] is this: "People are not willing to pay for a system that looks simpler because it looks less capable. Make the actual complexity low, the real simplicity high. That's an exciting design challenge: make it look powerful while also making it easy to use."

But like tic-tac-toe, the only real way to win the features game is to not play it. People want to feel that they are getting something—some value—for their money. This is what the value proposition is all about. In lieu of any other feeling—desire, joy, playfulness, luxury, and so on—people will turn to power, possibly out of fear. ("It's ugly as hell but at least this thing will work. I hope.") The feature list makes them—us—feel more comfortable with our choice.

The product strategy should instead focus on the story: how the product is not only what a set of users need, but also what they want to buy because it fits an empty space in the market—or creates a whole new market altogether. The features are there to support the story, not drive it.

---

3 "Feature Presentation" in *The New Yorker*, May 28, 2007. Online at www.newyorker.com/talk/financial/2007/05/28/070528ta_talk_surowiecki

4 In his article "Simplicity is Highly Overrated." Found online at www.jnd.org/dn.mss/simplicity_is_highly.html

Case Study: Wii

The Company

Nintendo, one of the world's largest video game companies.

The Problem

In the early 2000s, Nintendo faced a decision. Its high-end gaming console at the time, the Nintendo 64, was aging. It had been released in 1996, and Nintendo was watching its market share erode thanks to Sony's PlayStation and a new competitor in the space, Microsoft, with its Xbox console. In fact, in 2002, Microsoft pushed Nintendo down to third place in consoles sold in North America. Nintendo had to determine how it was going to compete in this increasingly challenging market.

The Process

Nintendo looked at the competitive landscape and determined that to challenge Xbox and PlayStation directly was a losing proposition. Those two gaming platforms were going head-to-head, feature-to-feature in the same market space, after the same audience. Instead, Nintendo focused their efforts on developing a product that would be played by those who didn't consider themselves "gamers": a market that Xbox and PlayStation had basically given up on. Its differentiator would be how its games would be played: with gesture-based controls.

The Solution

By focusing on the behavior the Wii engenders (playing a game in space), Nintendo opened up an entirely new market for gaming, and redefined the category in which it would have likely continued to lose ground had it simply released another console to compete directly with PlayStation and Xbox. While Nintendo still focused on hardware, it offered a strong value proposition by having a unique way of playing digital games that has been embraced by groups from the elderly (who hold Wii bowling tournaments) to small children: audiences who would never think to buy an Xbox or PlayStation.

The Wii has been an unqualified smash success and has become a worldwide phenomenon, winning countless awards and making billions of dollars in sales. In the first half of 2007 alone, the Wii sold more units in the United States than the Xbox 360 and PlayStation 3 combined, according to the NPD Group. In many countries, the Wii is now the top-selling game console. Sales are expected to surpass 50 million units sold in 2009, according to Nintendo, and demand, three years after its launch, is still incredibly high.

Pricing

The sister of features is pricing. At some point in the strategy process, someone is going to have to determine the **revenue model** for the product. Is it given away free? Sold as a subscription? A luxury item? A bargain item? Supported by advertising?

The **price point** is a significant piece of information, because it determines a lot of the decisions to be made during the design process and often during resourcing as well. There is often a significant difference—in both materials and the time allotted to design it—between a high-end, specialized product and a bargain, mass-market one.

How pricing is determined is a bit of a black art. Certainly, what competitors charge for a similar product will be a factor, but there are many other considerations as well. The **profit margin** has to be determined: how much profit does the company want versus the cost to design, manufacture, market, and support this product. Too much of a markup on a product and it could seem overpriced; too little and the product may not be worth creating.

Complicating this, some companies rely on volume of sales with low profit margins to increase their revenue (the cost leadership strategy described earlier), while some sell only a few items at high profit margins (the differentiation strategy). And increasingly, the products themselves are sold at a loss, with the services they hook into making up the difference (common in mobile phones, for example).

Designers may or may not have a say in pricing, but at a minimum they should be aware of the price point before embarking on the remainder of the design process.

Visualization and Visioning

Once you have the value proposition and the differentiators, it's time to start figuring out what the product might be like; to create a theoretical "shadow" product that embodies these characteristics. This is where visualization and visioning come into play.

One place where projects can get mired is in the strategy work. While it can be somewhat easy to find differentiators and determine the value proposition, it can be difficult to move past that into getting the go-ahead from

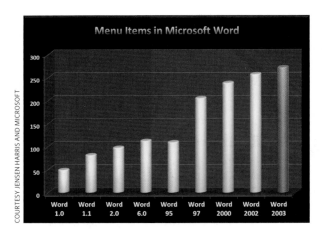

COURTESY JENSEN HARRIS AND MICROSOFT

Figure 3.4

Graphs like this one helped convince Microsoft management of the need for a radical overhaul of its Office suite (see the Case Study in Chapter 1).

stakeholders to create an actual project. This is where the designers' visualization (and persuasion) tools come into play. Using tools of communication design to visualize aspects of the design strategy (**Figure 3.4**) can motivate the organization into action.

Designers are capable of making the abstract into something tangible, and this is a skill that is used throughout the design process (see for example Chapter 5 on modeling research data). During design strategy, visualizations of the strategy and proposed project (**Figure 3.5**) can make for powerful tools of persuasion for the company to go ahead with the proposed project and to assign it enough resources (time, budget, and labor) to make it successful.

Visioning is where the creative synthesis of all the ideas that have accumulated through problem setting, stakeholder interviews, competitive analysis, and differentiation are given form. This is where parts of strategy can be articulated: success metrics, target market, value proposition, and differentiators. This where you lay out what the product you are about to design will be.

What you absolutely do not want to do is only present what is already known. There is little to no value in presenting data without some analysis of it, unless the organization is chaotic and needs to simply know what its own stakeholders said. But it is in the consolidation, analysis, and visualization of the collected information that designers demonstrate their value in strategy work.

In visioning, it's important to indicate how the organization will know if the project is successful. Visioning is also a good time to indicate **market segmentation**. That is, who are we targeting this product towards? Who are the expected customers and how many of them are there? What is their behavior, and how does it intersect with the proposed product? This information could be revised heavily after doing research (see Chapter 4), but knowing the likely customer base gives something to aim toward in research planning.

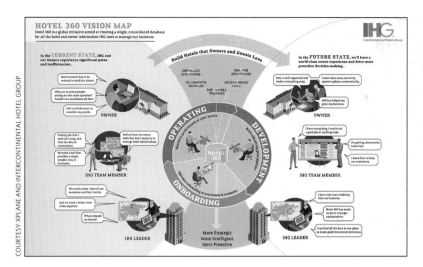

Figure 3.5

Hotel 360 is a common database and series of applications that provided one view of the data across the enterprise, replacing dozens of disconnected databases and applications that didn't talk to one another, causing great pain for owners and employees alike. This project helped IHG visualize the pains that existed in the current state, and the benefits of Hotel 360 in the future state.

Visualizations can take many different forms: from charts and graphs to storyboards to posters and presentations. The form of the visualization should be determined by the organization. That is, what does the organization best respond to? How do people in the organization communicate ideas? Using a familiar format to communicate an idea may help it be accepted. Then again, designers may want to avoid formats like spreadsheets and Word documents that are too easily ignored because they are so familiar. An unusual form can make a powerful statement by drawing attention and interest.

Vision Prototypes

One tool for visioning is the **vision prototype**. Vision prototypes are an imagination of what the final, polished design might look like (**Figure 3.6**). A faux screenshot, a CAD rendering, a movie or animation, or some sort of photorealistic image are usually what vision prototypes are. The purpose of a vision prototype is to make tangible what the end result might be and thus get stakeholder enthusiasm and organizational resources to start the design process.

COURTESY SOUNDFLAVOR

Figure 3.6

A vision prototype created during the strategy phase for Soundflavor's desktop application. Although the application changed considerably, the final form and feature set were highly influenced by this image.

Vision prototypes can be dangerous tools, however. You are showing what looks like a final design without going through any of the work to actually make the final design. Stakeholders could latch on to what is produced and expect that it *is* the final design. Radical changes (which are likely) in the design that occur over the course of the design process will need to be explained and justified as to why it is different from what was shown earlier in the process.

Project Planning and Roadmapping

Now that you understand the business objectives and environment, have defined the differentiators and value proposition, and envisioned the end state to get the stakeholders aligned, it's time to become tactical and figure out how to get the product made.

Almost every project is constrained by three things: time, budget, and manpower. Once a strategy is agreed upon, a project plan should be created (or at least reviewed) to more accurately determine how to allocate these resources appropriately.

Start by setting an end date. This also means finding out or determining the **market window**, or an estimation of how long there is before another competitor moves into the space, or the opportunity no longer exists because of other (economic/social/technological) forces. Once you have the end date, work backwards from there, blocking out time in chunks for the various portions of the design process: research and analysis, ideation, refinement, and prototyping. If you have a very limited amount of time, some of these steps will be severely truncated, if not eliminated from the process altogether. Some tips for allocating resources:

▸   If "the user" or "the customer" is ill-defined or being used as a strawman to justify any decision (especially conflicting decisions), you'll want to spend time to research user behavior (Chapter 4) to create personas (Chapter 5).

▸   If you are working in a different culture or context, or in an unfamiliar subject area, research and testing (Chapter 8) are practically necessities.

▶ If the business logic or constraints are challenging, leave time for use cases, functional specifications, and logic flows (Chapter 7).

▶ If the activity to be designed is complex and has multiple stages, leave extra time for alignment diagrams (Chapter 5), and task flows, scenarios, and storyboards (Chapter 7).

▶ If you are working on a product that combines hardware and software, build in integration time and checkpoints throughout ideation, refinement, and prototyping (Chapters 6–8).

▶ While it is difficult to determine at this point, if you suspect your product will have many different states or screens, leave extra time during refinement for storyboards and wireframes (Chapter 7).

▶ If you are working with new technology or on an unfamiliar platform, leave extra time for development and prototyping (Chapter 8).

The project plan should be created (possibly in a program like Excel or Microsoft Project) and posted somewhere where the team can see it (either physically or online). Key dates and associated deliverables should be made known and agreed to by the team and any essential stakeholders. A project plan could also call out things like cost, duration of each phase, dependencies, and feasibility of success.

It's important to note that the project plan will definitely change as the project goes on and more information about the product, its users, and the constraints are uncovered. The project plan should be considered a living document, although in many cases there is definitely a hard, fixed end date that cannot be changed.

Product Roadmap

Products have a lifecycle, and it is good to plot that out, as it might be unlikely to get every feature into an initial product release. Your product strategy is your opportunity to plan for the future, to create a **product roadmap**. A product roadmap is a document that outlines the evolution of a product over time. It details the set of features/technology/platforms/hardware upgrades that will be created or added over time.

For example, a digital camera might launch with a small set of features and no accessories. A second project creates accessories. A third project adds features. A fourth project designs the second generation of the camera with some accessories built in and better hardware. And so on.

Creating a product roadmap allows for organizations to smartly allocate resources to projects and to establish a long-term vision for a product. It can also help organizations to not try to do too much in a single product launch, which can cause the project never to launch.[5] They are also a good place to link back to the overall business strategy, to attach metrics and revenue targets to specific releases.

Summary

As Buckminster Fuller noted, "You never change things by fighting the existing reality. To change something, build a new model that makes the existing model obsolete." This is what the best strategies do: they create new demand and open up new spaces for products to live.

We now turn our attention to understanding the people who will use the products interaction designers create, and the contexts they will use them in.

For Further Reading

Blue Ocean Strategy: How to Create Uncontested Market Space and Make the Competition Irrelevant, W. Chan Kim and Renée Mauborgne

Subject To Change: Creating Great Products & Services for an Uncertain World, Peter Merholz, Todd Wilkens, Brandon Schauer, and David Verba

Building Design Strategy: Using Design to Achieve Key Business Objectives, Thomas Lockwood and Thomas Walton (eds.)

Creating Breakthrough Products: Innovation from Product Planning to Program Approval, Jonathan Cagan and Craig M. Vogel

Seeing Differently: Insights on Innovation, John Seely Brown (ed.)

Competitive Strategy: Techniques for Analyzing Industries and Competitors, Michael E. Porter

Managing the Design Factory, Donald G. Reinertsen

The Reflective Practitioner: How Professionals Think in Action, Donald A. Schön

Zag: The Number One Strategy of High-Performance Brands, Marty Neumeier

---

5 See, for instance, the infamous Chandler product, detailed in the book *Dreaming in Code* by Scott Rosenberg

4

Design Research

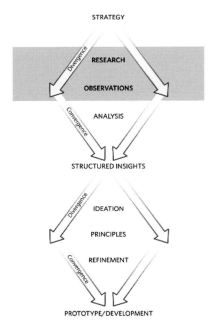

STRATEGY

RESEARCH

OBSERVATIONS

ANALYSIS

Divergence

Convergence

STRUCTURED INSIGHTS

IDEATION

PRINCIPLES

Divergence

REFINEMENT

Convergence

PROTOTYPE/DEVELOPMENT

Imagine a zoo where the zookeepers don't know anything about animals, and they don't bother to find out about the animals' natural habitat, dietary needs, or natural predators. The zookeepers keep the animals in metal cages, group the animals randomly together, and feed them whatever they have around. Now imagine the chaos that ensues and the unhappy (or worse: sick or dead) animals that would be the result. Not the type of place you'd want to take your kids to.

Our fictional zoo is the state of a lot of the products and services today, albeit not so extreme. While most businesses do have strong interest in their customers and put considerable amount of money into their products and services, a lot of that money is poorly spent. If only a small bit of the typical time, money, and resources used to make and market a product or service were put towards design research—observing, talking to, and maybe even making artifacts with customers and users—the products and services we use would be greatly improved.

What Is Design Research?

Design research is the act of investigating, through various means, a product's or service's potential or existing users and the context of use. Design research uses a hodgepodge of methods drawn from anthropology, scientific and sociological research, theater, and design itself, among other disciplines. The methods (some of which are detailed later in this chapter) range from silent observation to lively engagement with subjects in active play, such as role playing and model making.

Designers use these research methods to obtain information about the subjects and their environment that the designers might otherwise not have known and are thus better able to design for those subjects and environments. It behooves designers to understand the emotional, cultural, and aesthetic context that the product or service will exist in. Only through research can designers find out.

NOTE *When users are invited in throughout the design process for research purposes (to help generate ideas, discuss concepts, and test prototypes), it is often called participatory design (PD).*

Most design research is qualitative, not quantitative. **Qualitative research** is (arguably) more subjective, based on smaller, targeted sample sizes, and is concerned more with *how* and *why* questions. **Quantitative research**, on the other hand, is often about large, random, statistically-significant sample sizes and is designed to answer *what* questions. The outcome of quantitative research is often numerical data than can be made into statistics and mathematical models, while the outcome of qualitative research is usually interview videos, pictures, and other, "softer" data that is (again, arguably) more open to interpretation. Designers can, of course, do both, but this chapter will focus on qualitative methods of research, as those can focus more easily on motivations, expectations, and behaviors, and are thus most valuable to interaction designers.

Why Bother with Design Research?

Interaction designers aren't usually required to do design research. As noted in Chapter 2, many designers don't; instead, they trust their instincts, knowledge, and experience to create products. And in some cases, especially on small projects or in a subject area the designer knows well, this may be the correct approach. But on larger projects in unfamiliar domains, cultures, or subject areas, this approach can be risky. Without any up-front (sometimes called **generative**) research, designers risk finding out later in the process—during testing (see Chapter 8) or, worse, after the product launches—that the product they've designed doesn't meet users' needs or doesn't work in its environment. Research can help prevent these costly mistakes.

Designers usually work on projects outside of their area of expertise (design). The best way, aside from being an intuitive genius, of understanding people different from yourself and the environments they live and work in is to do research. Meeting even a single user will likely change one's perspective on a project. Spending a day observing someone do his or her job will give insights into that job that you would never get otherwise.

Design research can be especially helpful if the product contains features and functionality that are for specific types of users (often power users), who are doing specific types of work, work that the designer doesn't do. Sometimes conducting research is the only way to understand the nuances of a specific feature, as well as its importance to a specific group of users.

Design research helps give designers **empathy** with users. An understanding of the users and their environment helps designers avoid inappropriate choices that would frustrate, embarrass, confuse, or otherwise make a situation difficult for users.

Design research can also lead to moments of inspiration, such as when a research subject says something enlightening, or the environment suggests how a product might fit into it.

Brenda Laurel on Design Research

Brenda Laurel, Ph.D., is the chair of the Graduate Program in Design at California College of the Arts. She has written and edited several seminal interaction design books, including Computers as Theater, The Art and Science of Human-Computer Interaction, *and* Design Research.

Why is design research important?

Perhaps the single most pernicious sort of folly I have seen over nearly 30 years in the computer field is the belief on the part of engineers, designers, and marketing people that they "just know" what will work for their audience. For an extremely observant, experienced designer, this may indeed be true, but such people are exceedingly rare, and those who are most successful have "trained" their intuition by carefully observing and reaching deep understanding of certain kinds of people, cultures, and contexts. For the rest of us, that first "great idea" is usually a shot in the dark. Examining the idea to discover the hypotheses that are implicit in it gives the designer a platform for inquiry that will inform the project. It may also surprise and delight the designer.

Brenda Laurel on Design Research (*continued*)

Full-blown ideas for great, innovative products do not come from research subjects. The designer need not fear that engaging in research means that one is the slave of their findings. Design research includes the careful analysis of findings, turning them this way and that, looking for patterns. At the end of the day, well-designed research findings can spark the imagination of the designer with outcomes that could not have been dreamt of by either the research subjects or even the designer herself. Good design research functions as a spring-board for the designer's creativity and values.

You've said that good design needs to understand "deep, roiling currents of our dynamic culture." Is research the best method for divining those currents?

Well, "research" is a pretty broad term. Exploration, investigation, looking around, finding out are all synonyms for research. In the business of cultural production, exposure to popular media is essential research. Television, movies, news, games, nonfiction, science fiction—all facets of the Spectacle—can provide a great deal of information about the trajectories of change, what people long for and what they fear; what sorts of stories are told and why; how people are likely to greet particular changes in their world.

What should designers look for when doing research?

The dictionary definition frames research as "scholarly or scientific investigation or inquiry." The first step is to deliberately identify one's own biases and beliefs about the subject of study and to "hang them at the door" so as to avoid self-fulfilling prophecies. One must then frame the research question and carefully identify the audiences, contexts, and research methods that are most likely to yield actionable results. Those last two words are the most important: actionable results. Often, the success of a research program hangs upon how the question is framed.

You've said that design needs to be a more "muscular" profession. How can research help in that?

Research helps design to become a more muscular profession because knowledge is power. Identifying the deepest needs of our times and carefully examining the complexes of beliefs, practices, attitudes, hopes, and fears that surround them can empower designers to do more than embroider the Spectacle. Muscular design can lift the veil and open new pathways through the challenges that confront us, from the everyday challenge of opening a bottle of medicine with arthritic hands to the global challenge of designing everything for sustainability, increasing delight while decreasing the weight of the human footprint on Earth.

Research Planning

Doing research, especially a larger research project with multiple locations, requires some planning up front for it to be successful. That planning involves finding subjects to research and locations for research, and figuring out the activities and interview questions that will get you the information you need. In short, you need to figure out who you are going to research and what you are trying to find out.

Designers can help themselves focus by creating a **hunt statement** before going out into the field. A hunt statement is a tool for narrowing down what the designer is researching and why. Hunt statements typically take this form: I am going to research X so that I can do Y. X is often an activity, and Y is usually a project goal or subject area. Here's an example: I am going to research how doctors use laptops on the job so that I can design a laptop for them. Hunt statements should be developed before doing research so that there is a purpose to each piece of research. The more specific the hunt statement, the better.

Costs and Time

One myth of design research is that it is expensive and time consuming. And while it can be—some rare design research projects cost millions of dollars and take place over years—most design research takes place over days or weeks and costs in the tens of thousands of dollars. It is time and money well spent.

The materials necessary for design research can be as simple as a notebook and a pen, or as complicated as specialized software and video-recording equipment. Ideally, a research team will have two of everything: two notebooks, two cameras (in case one breaks), and four pens. The research team itself should consist of (at least) two people who can trade off interviewing and moderating duties during research sessions.

The amount of time spent doing research can vary widely. Even a single day spent doing research will improve the outcome of the project. Ideally, however, designers will want enough time to interview and observe a representative group of users. In most cases, this will be more than 10 people, but fewer than 40. Time needs to be set aside not only for doing the research itself, but also for recruiting subjects, which can be quite time consuming itself. Generally speaking, most design research takes from a week to two months to execute from beginning to end.

Recruiting

The validity of your research data is entirely dependent on finding the right subjects to research. Before going into the field, determine who you should be speaking to and then try to find them. This requires figuring out a set of characteristics of the people you want to speak to. These can include basics such as age, gender, geographic location, and other "marketing segmentation" type characteristics. It should also include behavioral criteria such as level of expertise, attitude toward the product, and frequency or likelihood of product use or activity engagement.

Unless your users (or prospective users) are an extremely narrow group, some diversity is essential in order to make sure you are getting valuable research data and enough variety of viewpoints and, especially, behavior. Be careful to avoid **unconscious bias** in choosing subjects. As humans, we often unconsciously choose to engage with people who appear similar to us. In design research, unconscious bias might keep you from valuable subjects with markedly different viewpoints.

Once you have the criteria, you should figure out the number of users you will need for each criterion. A good, basic rule of thumb is around four to six subjects per major characteristic. Of course, you can combine criteria into clusters, such as "women 18–30 who are current users," which can help with recruiting. It helps to have a spreadsheet to track which criteria remain to be recruited.

You should create a **screener** to help make sure you are getting the right people. A screener is a set of initial questions to make sure a subject is a good fit and matches all the criteria you need. You want to make the screener as specific as possible so that you get the right combination of subjects. The screener should not only ask characteristic questions ("Are you female?" "What is your age?" and so on) but also specific questions in the subject area to make sure that the potential subject isn't lying about what they know. There are people who participate in research studies strictly for the money, regardless of whether they are qualified, so it behooves you to try to root out those people before you waste your time researching them. If, for example, you are doing a project for active stock traders, you may want to ask potential subjects about common ticker symbols such as Microsoft (MSFT) just to make sure they really are who they say they are. It'll probably become obvious during research that a subject is an impostor, but it is far better to find this out during a screener than in the midst of an interview. In order to get a large number of potential subjects to choose from, you should disclose the incentive before asking potential subjects the criteria questions.

There are firms that will recruit research subjects when given a screener. Often companies will have a list of customers to recruit from that they can check the screener against. There are also ways to recruit subjects over the Web, using sites like Craigslist, or using a tool like Bolt|Peters' Ethnio (**Figure 4.1**) to intercept potential subjects at particular Web sites with an online screener.

Figure 4.1

Research subjects can be recruited online using tools such as Ethnio, which essentially let you present your screener as a Web site popup.

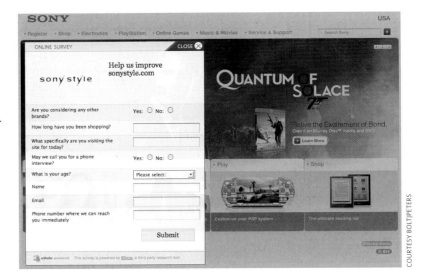

However it is done, recruiting takes time. You can expect, in some cases, for recruiting to take as much time as the actual research itself, especially if the subjects are difficult to find.

Moderator Script

In order to make sure you are getting good data, you need to ask the right questions, so it is best to create a moderator script before doing a research session. A moderator script guides the person or people running a research session (the moderators) on what to say and in what order to say it.

Moderator scripts (sometimes called discussion guides or protocols) should contain not only questions designed to entice the right data from a subject, but also instructions to the person conducting the research. Research sessions can be stressful, and it is easy to forget basic tasks like turning the video camera on, or resetting an activity. Writing down those instructions will help make the sessions run more smoothly.

When possible, moderators should avoid questions that can be answered with a yes or no; instead focus on drawing out stories and answers to how, what, and why questions: How is this activity done? Why is it done this way? What tools do you use to do it? If I took those tools away, how would you do it? And so on.

You should avoid leading questions ("So how good is this product?") and instead present as neutral and objective a tone as possible. Remember that the research subjects are people in the unfamiliar situation of being interviewed and observed. They want to give researchers what they want and will look to the researcher for cues as to what they should say and do. Thus, you can easily influence their responses through the phrasing of your questions ("Wasn't that a confusing widget?"). Revise questions that might suggest a given (your) answer.

The moderator script should be treated as a living, working document. After a few sessions have been run, it will likely become clear where the script has to be tweaked and refined, so moderators should do so. There is also usually no harm, unless it eats up all your session time, in deviating from the script to follow an interesting or revealing line of questioning. In fact, this is to be encouraged (within reason). However, make sure your goals remain consistent so you don't deviate from the point of the research—refer to the hunt statement if you need to.

Conducting Design Research

Anthropologist Rick E. Robinson[1] has outlined three main rules drawn from anthropology for conducting design research:

▶   **You go to them.** Designers shouldn't read other people's research on their research subjects from the comfort of their offices. Designers shouldn't make subjects come to them, to an artificial testing environment in an unfamiliar location. Observing the environment—where activities are performed—is an essential component of any research.

▶   **You talk to them.** Designers shouldn't just read about their subjects. Nor should they ask other people about them. Designers should have subjects tell their own stories in their own manner. The nuances of *how* a story is told can often tell a designer as much as the story itself.

▶   **You write stuff down.** The human memory is faulty. If designers can't write down what they see and hear directly as they do their research, then they should do so immediately afterward.

What Not to Do

Years of marketing methodology has left its mark. The first thing that most people think of when they think about talking to users is assembling a focus group. *Don't do this.* Focus groups are artificial constructs that, like juries, can be swayed and manipulated by strong participants in it, throwing off natural results. And that's to be expected—focus group facilitators assemble people into a synthetic group in an artificial setting (usually a conference room with a two-way mirror) and pepper them with scripted questions. This is not a good way to do design research. Rule #1: You go to them.

Nor is it a good idea to rely solely on the research of others, unless they are on the design team. Without knowing the circumstances and methods of the research, designers typically can't verify that the results are good and that they record the data that is most important to the designer: what the subjects did, said, or made, and the environment they were in. This dictum is especially true for data derived from marketing research. Marketing research typically focuses on demographics and attitudes—some of the least interesting data from a designer's point of view. Rule #2: You talk to them—emphasis on *you.*

---

1   See a collection of Robinson's papers and presentations online at www.rickerobinson.com

Designers shouldn't rely on a videotape or transcript to capture what they need to remember. Reviewing audio or videotape is a tedious process and will seldom be done, except to find specific moments. Transcripts of tapes, while useful, take time to create even when using a transcription service, and the designer may need the information before the transcript is complete. And there is always that dreadful possible moment when the video camera malfunctions. Designers need to take their own research notes, both for safety and to focus their observations. Rule #3: You write stuff down.

Ethical Research

When conducting research, designers should strive to treat their subjects ethically. Not only is this the right thing to do, but it will yield better results as well, since the subjects will likely open up more if they know and feel that they (and their data) are being treated well. Ethical research requires following these guidelines:

- ▶ **Get informed consent from subjects.** The designer should tell the subject that he or she is conducting a research study and explain the purpose. The subject must understand what is going on and agree to participate, preferably in writing. With studies involving minors, parental or guardian approval in writing is a necessity. An exception to this guideline is observations in public spaces where it would be impossible or impractical to get consent from everyone in view.

- ▶ **Explain the risks and benefits of the study.** Some studies carry with them risks. The designer may hear or see something that the subject doesn't want him to. The presence of a designer could be dangerous or make certain tasks cumbersome. But the designer should also explain what he or she hopes will improve as a result of the study ("We're going to build a better system for tracking shipments of ball bearings"), both to reassure the subject and to ensure good research results.

- ▶ **Respect the subjects' privacy.** Never use subjects' real names or other data that might identify them. Blur or hide faces in photographs. This will ensure that anything that subjects do or say won't have personal repercussions for them.

- ▶ **Pay subjects for their time.** People's time is valuable, and people who give some of it to provide insights to designers should be paid for it, at least a token amount. This payment doesn't necessarily have to be cash, although it should have value to the subjects.

▶   **If asked, provide data and research results to subjects.** Some subjects will want to see what you have recorded and the outcomes of the research. Designers should respect these requests.

What to Look For and How to Record It

When in the field, designers can get overwhelmed with the amount of data they are suddenly receiving. Often the designers are in a strange environment interacting with strangers. The newness of everything makes everything seem important. But the designer needs to focus on observing the things that are truly essential—namely, specific activities, the environment where activities take place, and the interactions among people that take place during activities.

Patterns and Phenomena

In the field, the main things a designer looks for are patterns and unique phenomena.

Patterns can be patterns of behavior, patterns in stories, patterns of responses to a question—any action or idea that keeps recurring. The rules of thumb are these:

▶   See or hear it once, it's a phenomenon. Write it down.

▶   See or hear it twice, it's either a coincidence or a pattern emerging. Write it down.

▶   See it or hear it three times, it's a pattern. Write it down.

Sometimes patterns won't emerge until after the research data has been analyzed (see Chapter 5). Sometimes a pattern is obvious in the midst of doing the research. Indeed, one good rule of thumb is that when you start noticing many patterns, you've likely done enough research to draw some meaningful conclusions.

Phenomena are interesting to a designer as well. Unusual behaviors—especially unusual methods of working—can suggest directions that will benefit larger numbers of people in their work. Say an accountant has created a different use for a spreadsheet; perhaps this approach can be built into the spreadsheet so that others can use it as well.

NOTE   *It's never a good idea to do research alone. Having a second pair of eyes, ears, and hands is immensely valuable for observing, listening, and recording, and for discussing and analyzing the research data afterwards. Two people observing the same phenomenon can draw (at least) two distinct conclusions from it, provided both saw it. Sometimes another person can be valuable simply to help capture the rich data being observed. Patterns can be subtle and easily missed.*

Field Notes

Writing down observations and key phrases is essential. Paper notebooks are best and less distracting than laptops or mobile devices, unless the environment is one where a notebook might seem more conspicuous, such as in an office environment.

All field notes should start the same way: recording the name of the person doing the research and the day, time, and place where the research is taking place. These details are crucial, especially for reference later in the project when these items can provide cues for recalling details. ("Remember that woman in the diner? The one we talked to last Tuesday. What did she say again?") Although the designer may record subjects' names and other data to provide compensation, for instance, this data should be kept separately from field notes, which should use pseudonyms instead of real names to preserve the anonymity of the subjects. Another thing to leave out, no matter how tempting, are personal opinions about the subjects, the observed activities, or overheard conversations. Doing otherwise is simply asking for trouble. Subjects, clients, and teammates may want to see the field notes, and showing bias in them is not only unprofessional, but bad research. Bias in research can't be helped, but it can (and should) be minimized.

It's a good idea, however, for the designer to have a separate area on the page to jot down thoughts and feelings that arise during the research sessions, including possible patterns. This should be a place to capture quick reflections or flashes of insight that can be explored more fully later.

Other findings that should be written down in the field notes are:

▹   Exact quotes with indications of emphasis and tone—Bob: "I sure do love these controls" (said ironically).

- ▶ Sketches of the location, annotated with comments and detail.

- ▶ The history, steps, and context of any activities.

Still pictures should be taken when and where feasible. Ideally, these will be printed, attached to the accompanying field notes, and annotated with captions or other notes. When taking pictures, make sure you are capturing not just the subject, but also the environment, any objects that are mentioned, and especially any activities being performed or demonstrated.

Research Methods

Design research has many methods, drawn from other disciplines or created by designers over the years. These methods can be roughly divided into three categories: observations, interviews, and activities, including having subjects make things and self-report on their activities.

Whole books have been written on the methods of design research (see For Further Reading at the end of the chapter), so what follows is a representative sample of the most common methods.

Observations

The easiest and possibly the most fruitful of all design research methods is simply observing what people are doing in a conscientious manner. Designers can covertly watch or interact with people or tag along with subjects to ask them questions about how and why they are doing what they are doing.

- ▶ **Fly on the wall.** Go to a location and unobtrusively observe what goes on there. For instance, a designer could go to a mall and watch how people shop.

- ▶ **Shadowing.** Follow subjects as they go about their routines. This technique usually requires permission, as the designer is following the subject throughout the day, recording what is done and said.

- ▶ **Contextual inquiry.** A variation on shadowing, contextual inquiry involves going to the subjects' location and asking questions about their behaviors, such as "Why are you doing that? Could you describe that to me?"

▶   **Undercover agent.** Observe people by interacting with them covertly, posing as someone "normal" in the environment. A designer who wants to know about a service can pretend to be a customer and use the service.

When conducting observations, dress not to impress. The point is to blend in with the environment so that the observer isn't the one being observed. Observers should wear neutral, nondescript clothing that is appropriate to the environment. The more observers look like they belong, the more they'll become part of the background. Bring props if necessary. Some environments require certain items for the observer to seem normal, such as a backpack in school settings, a hard hat on construction sites, or a suit in a conservative office.

Observers should choose their locations wisely and be willing to change to another one if the original doesn't seem to be yielding good results. Observers should sit or stand in places where they can observe without being noticeable. It's best to be at an angle when observing subjects instead of directly in front or back of them, because an angle gives a clearer line of sight.

Camera phones are excellent for inconspicuously snapping photos in public spaces. Remember, however, that any such photos should be used in an ethical manner.

Interviews

It's amazing what you can find out if you just ask. Talking to people and hearing their stories is a great way to uncover attitudes and experiences—but designers do need to be careful: what people say they do and what they actually do are typically two very different things. Here are some methods for talking to users:

▶   **Directed storytelling.** Ask subjects to tell stories about specific times they performed an action or interacted with a product or service. Moments to ask about are the first time they performed an action or used a product ("Tell me about the first time you used the system to place an order"), a time when the product or service hasn't worked ("Can you describe a time when you couldn't do something you wanted to with your mobile phone?"), and a time when they did something new ("Why did you try to use the screwdriver to pry open the phone?").

▶   **Unfocus group.** A method from design firm IDEO,[2] this approach turns the traditional focus group on its head. Instead of assembling a group of users in a room to talk about a subject or product, this method suggests assembling a group of experts in the field, hobbyists, artists, and others to explore the subject or product from different viewpoints. The purpose is not to get a typical user's perspective, but instead an atypical view of the subject.

▶   **Role playing.** With a willing group or individual, role playing different scenarios can draw out emotions and attitudes about a subject, product, or service in ways that can be very fresh ("I'm going to pretend I'm a customer and interact with you. Is that okay?").

▶   **Extreme-user interviews.** Another method from IDEO, in this approach the designer interviews people on the outer edge of the subject matter. For example, a designer working on an interactive TV project might interview a subject who doesn't own a TV.

Figure 4.2

A desk tour can reveal how people structure their personal space to work and uncover objects and methods users neglected to mention.

▶   **Desk/purse/briefcase tour.** Ask subjects to give a tour of their desks or the contents of their purses or briefcases (**Figure 4.2**). How people use their desks and what they carry with them can reveal a lot about their personalities and work habits. Are they messy or neat? Organized or disorganized? Do they have special systems for working? Are there family pictures?

When talking to subjects, it's best to have what Buddhists call the "beginner's mind." Designers should be open and nonjudgmental and should not assume that they know the answer beforehand. Simple questions can reveal powerful answers.

---

2 See IDEO's method cards for more. www.ideo.com/work/item/method-cards/

Activities

A recent trend in design research calls for designers to not only observe and talk to users, but also to have them engage in an activity that involves making an artifact. This process allows designers to draw out emotions and understand how people think about a subject. Doing activities frees subjects' creativity and allows them to express themselves differently than they would in an interview. Here are some methods for making artifacts with subjects:

Figure 4.3

Creating collages can give visual and verbal clues as to how subjects think and feel about a topic.

- ▶ **Collaging.** Using images and words, have subjects make a collage related to the product or service being researched (**Figure 4.3**). For a mobile phone project, for example, designers might have subjects make a collage on mobility. The collage images can come from magazines, the Web, or stock photographs, and should contain a wide range of subjects and emotions. The same is true for the words. About 200 words, both positive and negative, should be printed out on strips of paper for use. Subjects should have a way to write their own words as well.

- ▶ **Modeling.** Using modeling clay, pipe cleaners, Styrofoam blocks, cardboard, glue, and other modeling tools, designers can have subjects design their version of a physical or even digital product. For example, a designer could have gamers design their ultimate game console or have air traffic controllers design an ideal set of controls.

- ▶ **Draw your experience.** Give subjects drawing materials and paper and tell them to draw their experience with a product or service (**Figure 4.4**). A project about e-mail, for example, might have subjects draw the lifecycle of e-mail on their computers.

Figure 4.4

Drawing experiences can bring out subjects' hidden experiences and emotions.

An important part of having subjects make things is having them explain their choices after they are done (**Figure 4.5**). Otherwise, the designer may be left with a perplexing object and no way of understanding it. Ask, for instance, why a subject chose negative words in the collage or why a subject built the robot that way. However, for the best results, designers shouldn't tell subjects beforehand that they will be explaining their choices; this could inhibit them as they complete the activity.

Making artifacts requires more advance preparation than other forms of research. Designers need to gather and choose the materials for making the artifacts as well as the tools to do so.

Figure 4.5

An essential part of having subjects make artifacts is having the subjects explain their choices afterwards.

Self-Reporting

Another type of activity is self-reporting. In this approach, subjects, not the researcher, record their activities and thoughts, and the researcher then collects and analyzes these records after the subjects are done. Self-reporting is an excellent tool for longer studies in multiple locations, when it would be impractical to send designers to do all of the research in person. Self-reporting can also be good for documenting moments that subjects might be reluctant or embarrassed to present to a designer in person. Self-reporting methods include the following:

▶ **Journals.** Subjects keep a journal of particular activities. A classic example is the journals kept by the Nielsen families, who write down what they watch on TV for two week's time so that the Nielsen ratings can be compiled.

▶ **Beeper studies.** Subjects wear a beeper, which the designer sets off during the day. When the beeper goes off, the subjects record in a journal what they are doing at that time.

► **Photo/video journals.** Subjects are given cameras and told to document activities and their daily lives. Research on dining experiences, for instance, might ask subjects to document every time they cook or eat something.

Self-reporting requires a lot of time and effort from the subjects, so the subjects should be selected (and compensated) accordingly.

Summary

Design research is a powerful tool in the interaction designer's toolkit. It allows designers to get away from their desks and out into the field where the product will be actually used. It can bring insights and inspiration that can change not only the end product, but even the strategy as well. New markets and new opportunities can be found, and the designer becomes immersed in the subject matter.

But, as Jesse James Garrett noted in his essay *ia/recon,*[3] "Research can help us improve our hunches, but research should inform our professional judgment, not substitute for it."

But research alone is almost useless. At the end of the research period, you have a pile of observations and data that are mostly unformed and not particularly helpful. The research data needs to be analyzed and turned into structured findings. Without the critical next step, what you've seen and heard will likely not make its way into the product. Research analysis and the making of structured findings are the subject of the next chapter.

For Further Reading

Design Research: Methods and Perspectives, Brenda Laurel and Peter Lunenfeld (eds.)

A Designer's Research Manual: Succeed in Design by Knowing Your Clients and What They Really Need, Jennifer Visocky O'Grady and Kenneth Visocky O'Grady

---

[3] Found online at www.jjg.net/ia/recon/

Observing the User Experience: A Practitioner's Guide to User Research, Mike Kuniavsky

Understanding Your Users: A Practical Guide to User Requirements, Catherine Courage and Kathy Baxter

Through Navajo Eyes: An Exploration in Film Communication and Anthropology, Sol Worth and John Adair

Learning From Strangers: The Art and Method of Qualitative Interview Studies, Robert S. Weiss

The Ethnographer's Toolkit, Volumes 1–7, by Margaret Diane LeCompte and Jean J. Schensul

5

Structured Findings

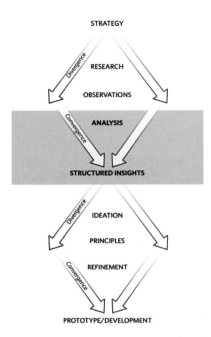

Notes. Pictures. Audio and video recordings. Impressions. Observations. These are the types of data that designers are typically left with after doing design research. Data like this can be worse than useless; it can be overwhelming and confusing. It needs to be turned into something that designers— and indeed, the whole product team and stakeholders—can understand and use. The unstructured mass of data needs to become **structured findings**.

Structured findings are research data put into a form that can be easily understood. They can be stories, models, visualizations, personas—anything that makes the unfiltered data into something helpful and actionable.

All the design research in the world is useless if it does not make its way into the hearts, minds, and hands of the design team and into the product itself. For that, analyzing the research in order to make structured findings is essential. It's astounding how often this crucial step is overlooked.

Preparing the Data

Before your research data can make sense, it needs to be analyzed. The first task of analysis is to see what you have.

Make the Data Physical

Usually, the research data will be fragmented and will exist in any number of places (laptops, notebooks, cameras, and so on), in a variety of for-

Figure 5.1

After gathering data, the next step is to make the data physical by putting important quotes, pictures, and sketches up on walls.

mats, from scrawled analog notes and drawings to hours of videotape. All that data needs to be collected and put into some sort of format so that the essential parts of it can be found, examined, and evaluated. The best way to do this is to make the data physical and visual. Print out photos and stills from video. Put important quotes on sticky notes (**Figure 5.1**).

Pull out key moments from transcripts and print those out large enough to be read from across the room.

The purpose of making everything visual and physical is to be able to draw connections across various pieces of data, and that can be hard to do unless you see the data, and can in some way physically manipulate it. If everything is printed out or put on sticky notes, it is an easy task to put pictures together, or to combine quotes and sketches. It removes the artificial barrier created by the disparate formats, applications, and locations of the initial data.

Making the data physical also allows you to unconsciously process the data while doing other tasks. Working while surrounded by images and quotes can lead to unexpected insights and connections.

Putting data up on the walls creates another powerful byproduct in the asynchronous conversation that takes place among the various viewers of the data. As people sit in the room or walk by, they too can make connections, even if they aren't part of the project!

It helps to have a permanent space for the research analysis work, where the data can be posted for a reasonable period of time—and perhaps even until the project concludes. If you don't have a physical space (sometimes called a project room, or project war room), you can post the data on large sheets of cardboard or foamcore so that they can be moved from room to room and stored when not in use.

Manipulating the Data

Once the data is visual and physical, it's time to play with it. Manipulating the data involves:

- Clustering similar pieces of data
- Combining/collapsing redundant pieces of data (**aggregation**)
- Juxtaposing related pieces of data
- Naming the resulting data clusters
- Juxtaposing *unrelated* pieces of data

This last activity is important, yet often overlooked. Putting two unlike items together forces the mind to find a connection between them—a story, a framework, a metaphor—and that connection can spark an insight. See **Figure 5.2**.

COURTESY PETE WENDEL AND GEONETRIC

Figure 5.2

Manipulating data for a hospital registration process. Note the connections being made between the clusters via simple marker.

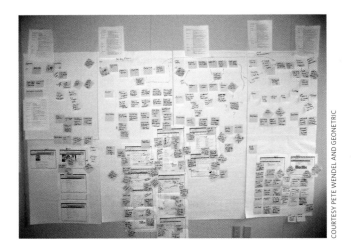

As with research itself, when manipulating the data, you are mainly looking for patterns. Pieces of data that seem related can form a pattern, and patterns are ultimately what structured findings are comprised of.

Sorting Data

Some standard ways of organizing data are:

- Alphabetical
- Numerical
- Chronological
- By frequency
- By subject (**Figure 5.3**)

Information designer Richard Saul Wurman laid out, in his 1989 book *Information Anxiety,* a set of categories to help organize data: Location, Alphabetical, Time, Category, Hierarchy—also known by their acronym LATCH or as the "Five Hat Racks" for hanging data onto. Location can be physical locations, or other kinds of socio-psychological spaces (for example, "Meditating"). Alphabetical is good for large pools of data of the same type, such as books or names. Time works well for any activities done in a sequence or over time. Categories refer to sorting by similar objects/types. Hierarchy is for when you want to assign value to the data: common to uncommon; big to small; expensive to cheap; important to inessential, and so on.

COURTESY RACHEL POWERS AND VISDE

Figure 5.3

Research on hearing aids, sorted by subject.

Another common mnemonic device for sorting data is AEIOU: Actions, Environment, Interactions, Objects, Users.

As you begin making structured findings, the data will continue to be manipulated in space, creating what will likely become conceptual models by the end of the analysis process.

Analyzing the Data

It's now time to begin the actual process of data analysis. There are four major ways to go about analyzing the data:

▶ Analysis

▶ Summation

▶ Extrapolation

▶ Abstraction

Each takes the data and transforms it in some way, either breaking it down into pieces (analysis), summarizing it, or creating something new with it (extrapolation, abstraction).

Remember that the end goal is not the research analysis itself, but rather the structured findings you can use to explain what the research discovered and why it's important.

Analysis

Analysis, a term for the general process, can also apply to how you examine the data. Analysis is the deconstruction of a whole process, activity, object, or environment into its component parts (which themselves can be deconstructed into their component parts). Each part can then be examined in order to discover its properties and characteristics.

Analysis tends to generate models such as flows and timelines that break a whole process down into its moments.

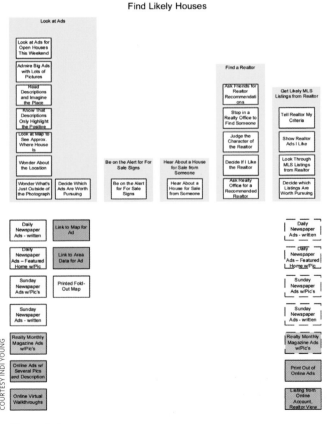

Alignment Diagram

One model that can come from analysis is an **alignment diagram** (**Figure 5.4**). An alignment diagram breaks a process down into its discrete steps, then indicates the problems and issues with each step, as well as the tools available to help users complete that stage of the activity.

Alignment diagrams are excellent for breaking down complex tasks and figuring out where the problems and opportunities lie within the process. Alignment diagrams make it easy to see where users have crucial decisions or activities, but no tool to help them perform it. These unsupported moments can be excellent design opportunities.

Figure 5.4

A small piece of a 70″-long alignment diagram (also known as "mental models") for buying a house. The activities are on the top of the diagram, while the tools to aid the activities are shown below.

Touchpoint List

Another type of analysis is a list of all the touchpoints. In services, **touchpoints** are the raw materials designers have to work with or need to create. For example, when checking in at an airport, the touchpoints include the human agent, the kiosk, the ticket itself, the ticket sleeve, and the counter.

These touchpoints can include (and certainly aren't limited to) any of the following:

▶ Physical locations

▶ Specific parts of locations

▶ Hardware

▶ Software

▶ Signage

▶ Objects

▶ Web sites

▶ Mailings (e-mail and regular)

▶ Spoken communication

▶ Printed communications (receipts, maps, tickets, and so on)

▶ Applications

▶ Machinery

▶ Customer service

▶ Partners

Do these exist already or do they need to be created? Are they well designed or are they trouble spots? A touchpoint map can show all the pieces of a service.

Process Map

Similar to an alignment diagram is a **process map** (**Figure 5.5**). A process map shows a high-level view of a service, its discrete steps, and, importantly, which part of the overall service is being worked on. A process map shows the boundaries of the project; it can also show the surrounding steps that are not going to be designed, or that might be affected by changes made during the course of a project. For instance, designing a check-in service at the airport might affect baggage claims, customer service, online reservations, and so on.

Process maps should also indicate the touchpoints at each stage of the process.

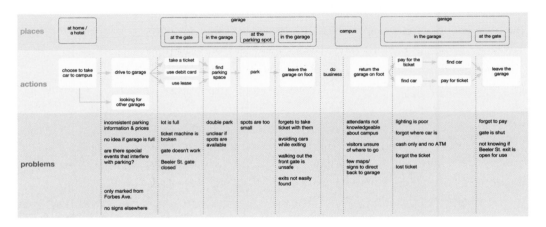

Figure 5.5

Process maps provide an overview of what parts of a service are to be designed and can indicate problem areas in an existing service.

Task Analysis

Another standard model that can be derived from research analysis is a task analysis. A **task analysis** is a raw list of activities that the final design will have to support. For example, imagine designing a new Web browser. Users will need to be able to:

▶   Go to pages by manually entering an address.

▶   Go to pages via a bookmark.

▶   Add a bookmark.

▶   Delete a bookmark.

▶   Organize bookmarks into folders.

▶   Print pages.

▶   Refresh a page.

▶   Return to the previous page.

▶   And so on, all the way down to rare and obscure tasks (for most users), such as viewing page source code and opening a JavaScript console.

Task analyses can be documented in spreadsheets or Word documents. They can also be mapped to wireframes (see Chapter 7) to indicate what tasks are being performed on each page. Tasks can be categorized by function, level of access required (basic user tasks, registered user tasks, administrator tasks, and so on), or even by persona (see later in this chapter) performing the task.

Task analysis is especially useful later in the design process as a check to see whether the design supports all the tasks required. Rare but important tasks often get overlooked, but with a task analysis, the designer can make sure the design meets all the requirements.

Summation

Taking pieces of data and making them add up to a conclusion is called **summation**. By summarizing, you create a more succinct piece of data that encapsulates a larger set of raw data in some way, and, importantly, characterizes it in some way, not just aggregates it.

Summation can be done on a micro level, such as describing a video tape ("Subject tries to use the kiosk and gives up") or at a macro level ("Every person we spoke to hated using this product").

Summation is also a good place to mix in quantitative data (numbers). For example, noting that 75 percent of research subjects did a particular activity can be a powerful piece of persuasion to demonstrate the need to support that activity.

Environment Description

Summations don't necessarily have to be in words and numbers alone. Maps, screenshots, diagrams, and even videos can be used for summation as well. Especially before starting the design of a service, designers need to know as much as they can about where the service will be located (or is located already). An **environment description** attempts to detail the location as much as possible. Photographs with annotations (**Figure 5.6**) are excellent for environment descriptions that summarize data.

Figure 5.6

Annotated
photographs from a
project done with the
Carnegie Library of
Pittsburgh by MAYA.

COURTESY MAYA

Extrapolation

Related to summation but taking it one step further, extrapolation is the creation of something new that can be suggested by (but is not a summary of)
existing pieces of data. **Extrapolation** is the opposite technique of analysis:
analysis seeks to break a whole into its parts; extrapolation seeks to make
a new, different whole from disparate parts. In a sense, all design based on
research is an extrapolation; the designer extrapolates a product from what
she knows about the users.

The most likely structured finding from extrapolation is a story or narrative. The story can take pieces of data and make them into either something nearly-known like a Day In The Life-type narrative, which "fills in
the blanks" between pieces of data to give a snapshot of a user's day, or the
designer can make a future story about how the product is going to fit into
what's now known about users' lives. Since the details of the product aren't
yet defined (see Chapter 7), this scenario will likely be broad, less focused
on the product itself and more on how it might affect the lives of users.

Abstraction

The fourth major way of analyzing data is by abstracting it so that it can be better understood. Abstraction involves removing data until only the most relevant data points remain. Those data points can be visualized as conceptual models.

By abstracting data, you not only remove a lot of noise caused by all the details data typically has, but you can then create a visual representation of the remaining data, which can be a powerful tool. Much like the strategic visualization discussed in Chapter 3, research visualizations can be shown to stakeholders and team members in order to educate, persuade, and validate the design and research.

With abstraction, there is always a fear of distorting the data, or even making it harder to comprehend through poor visuals, so designers need to make the data set as small as possible, and the resulting visuals as clear and uncluttered as possible.

Conceptual Models

The outcome of abstraction is usually a **conceptual model**. Conceptual models, in the words of Rick E. Robinson, are "things to think with." They are visual tools that allow the most relevant pieces of data to be surfaced and considered in a new light. They are ways of visualizing data so that, as in extrapolation, the sum of the parts adds up to something new. See **Figure 5.7**.

Figure 5.7

Perhaps the most famous conceptual model of all time is James Watson and Francis Crick's DNA model.

Conceptual models shouldn't be lists or bullet points. Instead, they should be visually appealing pieces of graphic design, memorable by themselves, that can then be examined, understood, and internalized.

Conceptual models make excellent **boundary objects**.[1] A boundary object is an item that exists in multiple communities at once, so that there is

---

1   For more on boundary objects see *Sorting Things Out: Classification and Its Consequences* by Geoffrey C. Bowker and Susan Leigh Star

common understanding between them of a particular subject. Conceptual models, done well, can do that between various internal departments and between designers and clients.

The best models of design research show (either implicitly or explicitly) three things:

> ▶   **Pain points.** Where are there difficulties in the process? What don't users like? What is creating unnecessary effort? What is inefficient or unpleasant?

> ▶   **Opportunities.** What are the opportunities for improvement? Where is a tool missing that might help users? What areas have been neglected that could be improved?

> ▶   **Calls to action.** What needs to be done in order to ameliorate the pain points and capitalize on the opportunities? What are the big design tasks that need to be done?

For example, **Figure 5.8** was created from data collected by talking to users of an intranet. The data revealed that much of the intranet, even features that users said they wanted, wasn't being used. Part of the reason these features were unused was because users didn't know they existed—they were buried in the system. The calls to action were clear: move the lines, so that more of the system was known and liked.

Figure 5.8

An example of a model derived from research. The designers discovered that most of the features of an intranet were unknown and unused, and those that were known and used were mostly disliked.

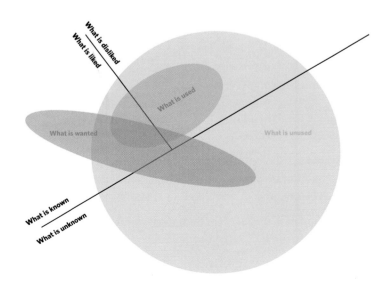

All of this information could, of course, be explained in words, as in the preceding paragraph, or shown in a statistical table. But neither of these would have the same impact as the model. Models become design tools, to be referred to repeatedly throughout a project. In this example, the designers could easily see and demonstrate to the client that a key problem is that the users can't find the features they want to use, even when the features already exist in the system.

These are the most common tools for representing research data:

▷ **Linear flow.** Shows how a process unfolds over time (**Figure 5.9**). Linear flows are good for showing designers where problems exist in a process.

▷ **Circular flow.** Shows how a process repeats itself in a loop (**Figure 5.10**). Circular flow is similar to a linear flow, except the process (or points in the process) repeat themselves.

▷ **Spider diagram.** Shows connections between data points. A piece of data is placed in the center of a diagram, and other data radiates out from it (**Figure 5.11**).

▷ **Sets.** Shows relationships between data points. (**Figure 5.12**).

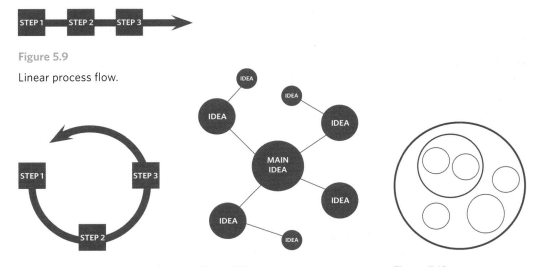

Figure 5.9
Linear process flow.

Figure 5.10
Circular process flow.

Figure 5.11
Spider diagram.

Figure 5.12
Sets diagram.

▸   **Venn diagram.** Similar to sets, uses overlapping circles to show connected relationships (**Figure 5.13**). Figure 5.8 is also a Venn diagram.

▸   **2x2 matrix.** Shows the relationship between data based on where the data points fall on two axes. These two axes separate data into four quadrants based on two simple variables (**Figure 5.14**).

▸   **Map.** Shows spatial relationships (**Figure 5.15**).

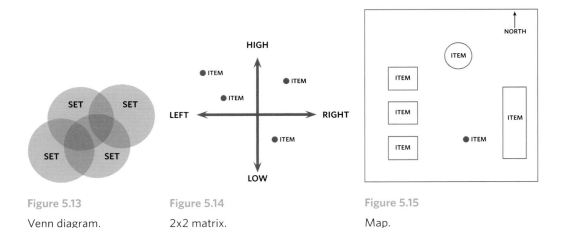

Figure 5.13

Venn diagram.

Figure 5.14

2x2 matrix.

Figure 5.15

Map.

Usually, the data itself suggests the correct way to display it. If, for example, the designer observes a step-by-step process that repeats, a circular flow makes sense to use.

Personas

A **persona** is a particular type of conceptual model, used for demarcating users by behavior, motivations, and expectations. Personas (**Figure 5.16**) are a documented set of archetypal people who are involved with a product or service. They're supposed to give designers a sense that they are designing for specific people, not just "the users," who, if ill-defined, can be twisted to serve any purpose. ("Of course the users will want to enter a password on every page!")

Dave
the information jockey
primary persona

information usage
info Names, Phone Numbers, Ideas
paper Notebook, Post-Its
info access 3-5x/day
# of locations/day 5
% mobile 35
mobile locations Subway, Street

"If I'm not connected,
I feel like I'm missing
something."

demographics
age 29
occupation Lawyer
location New York City
marital status Single
children None
income $135,000
education Graduated Law School
hobbies Working Out, Cooking

device usage
computer Sony VIAO Laptop
cell phone Sony Ericcson
pda CLIE
other Network Walkman
primary device Laptop
comfort Comfortable
web 50 hours/week
phone 10 hours/week
programs Email, Word, Excel, IE

Figure 5.16

A sample persona. Personas turn "the users" into identifiable human beings.

Designers devise personas from observing and talking to users. Personas are typically amalgams of multiple people who share similar goals, motivations, and behaviors. The differences between each persona must be based on these deep characteristics: what people do (actions and behaviors), what their expectations are, and what their reasons are (goals and motivations).

What personas shouldn't be are users who share common demographics. Focusing on demographics will provide market segments, not personas. The only time demographics really matter for personas is when those demographics directly affect user behavior. A 13-year-old will probably use a product differently than an 83-year-old. A rural peat farmer in Ireland might use a product differently than a Korean financial analyst in Seoul. But maybe not —demographics may not matter at all. In fact, using demographics could limit and hinder the usefulness of the personas. For products with millions of users, for example, a designer could end up with hundreds of personas, and such a large set is essentially useless.

To create a persona, designers find a common set of behaviors or motivations among the people they have researched. This becomes the basis for the persona, which should be given a name, a picture, and a veneer of demographic data to make the persona seem like a real person.

For example, consider a design project related to airline travel. Designers have observed three types of travelers: those flying frequently for business, those flying occasionally for pleasure, and those flying habitually every fall and spring (the snow bird phenomenon). Each of these overall behaviors is tied to specific detailed behaviors, expectations, and motivations while traveling. These characteristic become the basis for three personas: Bob, the frequent flier; Susan, the vacationer; and Wilma, the snow bird.

Quotes pulled from the research are helpful for distinguishing and identifying personas ("I fly at least once a week"), as are simple titles ("The Frequent Flier"). The persona documents should clearly note the behaviors, motivations, and goals that differentiate one persona from another. Bob cares deeply about getting to his meeting or hotel on time, while Wilma is more relaxed about what happens after the flight.

For most projects, the number of personas should be small—anywhere from one to nine. After about 10 personas, remembering and distinguishing them becomes difficult. Most important, it becomes difficult to design for such a large group. Imagine creating a mobile phone that will satisfy a dozen very different people. The "debate" that would go on among the personas would make it difficult for the designer to accomplish anything. Unless you are designing for millions of users, you should consolidate personas to fewer than 10. While both designer and client will usually want the product or service to work for the largest possible group, nine personas should be enough to cover 95 percent of the users. A product or service that is being designed to accommodate more personas likely isn't focused enough.

Once you have a set of personas, find a face for each. Pictures, more than anything else, will humanize personas and make them memorable. As long as the personas won't be made public, an online dating service like Yahoo Personals is an excellent place to find persona pictures. Personals contain (mostly) flattering pictures that can be browsed by any combination of gender, location, age, ethnicity, and other factors.

Personas by themselves are fairly useless. They become useful only when the designer sets up scenarios and uses the personas to test features for appropriateness and utility. Designers can then ask themselves: Would this persona do this task? Could this persona do this task as it is designed?

Designers (and, indeed, businesses) can also use personas to set priorities. The persona that represents a majority of a product's users may not be the user that the organization values the most; other personas may make the organization more money, be more involved, use more features, and so on. Organizations can and should use personas to make strategic decisions.

While many find personas helpful, some designers don't care for them. For these designers, personas form an artificial barrier between the product and its users. Some projects, especially smaller ones, may not warrant a full set of personas. But for most, if they are based on research and focused on the right characteristics (behaviors, motivations, and expectations), personas are a valuable tool.

Robert Reimann on Personas

Robert Reimann is an associate creative director at frog design and was the first president of the Interaction Design Association. He helped write the book on interaction design—literally, with Alan Cooper and David Cronin: About Face 3: The Essentials of Interaction Design.

How did the idea of personas come about?

The idea of personas, or tools like them, has been around for a long time. Many design, marketing, and usability professionals in the '80s and '90s made use of "user profiles" to help them visualize who their customers were, and to help them imagine what kind of needs and desires they might have in relation to products and services.

Alan Cooper, who coined the term "persona" for this type of tool, first did so in 1983, while designing and developing a software package called SuperProject for Computer Associates, and later did so for what eventually became Microsoft's Visual Basic.

Cooper's early personas were primitive, in that they were based on loose, personal observations of a small number of individuals in particular roles. However, Cooper's fundamental insight was that these representative characters had goals and behaviors that could be served by products. By enumerating the most critical goals and including them as part of the persona description, Cooper developed a powerful design method: meet the persona's top goals with the product by designing for their behaviors, and the design is much more likely to be successful.

Robert Reimann on Personas *(continued)*

My own contribution to Cooper's persona methodology was to introduce more formal ethnographic field research as the data-gathering method for the information used to construct personas, and to (with Kim Goodwin) refine the persona goals into three types: *experience goals*, which describe how users wish to feel (or not to feel) when using a product; *end goals*, which describe what users actually want or need to accomplish with a product to meet their expectations; and *life goals*, which describe the broader aspirations of the persona in relation to the product, and thus help describe what the product *means* to the persona. It's this focus on goals and behavior patterns, combined with a scenario-based method of translating these requirements into design solutions, that makes Cooper's personas so unique and powerful.

What are personas good for?

Personas are terrific tools for understanding and communicating user behaviors, needs, desires, and contexts. They are extremely useful for:

1. Directing the product design. Persona goals and behaviors inform both the structure and behavior of a product and its interface.

2. Communicating design solutions to stakeholders. Using personas in storyboards and scenarios is a very effective way to tell the story of the product and helps highlight why design decisions were made as they were.

3. Building consensus and commitment around the design. Having a common language around which the team can communicate regarding priorities and features and tying each decision specifically to user benefits/consequences helps rally a team to work together to make the best possible product for its target users.

4. Measuring the design's effectiveness. Design choices can be tested against persona behaviors, contexts, and expectations while they are still on the whiteboard, far in advance of testing on prototypes or final products. The result is better quality earlier in the design process, which makes later refinements more manageable.

5. Contributing to nondevelopment efforts. The information captured in personas and storyboards can be of great interest and use to marketing, advertising, sales, and even strategic planning activities within companies.

Robert Reimann on Personas *(continued)*

What are the essential components of any persona?

The most important elements of any persona are the behavior patterns gathered via ethnographic research and analysis, and the goals that derive from them. Furthermore, it is important to understand the persona's importance: for example, is it a primary persona (main design target), a secondary persona (served by an interface directed at the primary persona, but with some special additional requirements), or a persona that is not served by the product at all? In addition to these components, a representative name, a picture, and a small amount of additional demographic information helps make the persona seem real and engages stakeholder empathy. Personas must seem like credible, real people to maximize their effectiveness as design and development tools.

Summary

Designer Joan Vermette said, "My personal creative process is to construct a big, tall scaffold of theory and evidence, and then once that is built I get on my hang-glider-of-intuition and jump off the top of the scaffold. I seem to need to do a lot of thinking and testing before I let myself fly. But fly I do, eventually. And the scaffold is about the flying, actually."[2]

The last three chapters have been about building the scaffold, about making sure the product meets the needs of the organization and of the users. The next three chapters show how the product itself is conceived, refined, prototyped, and developed.

For Further Reading

Visual Explanations: Images and Quantities, Evidence and Narrative, Edward R. Tufte

The Visual Display of Quantitative Information, 2nd edition, Edward R. Tufte

Visualizing Data, William S. Cleveland

How to Lie with Statistics, Darrell Huff

---

2 On the Interaction Design Association mailing list. Quote can be viewed here: http://lists. whatwg.org/pipermail/discuss-interactiondesigners.com/2007-August/019765.html

Information Dashboard Design: The Effective Visual Communication of Data, Stephen Few

Designing for the Digital Age: How to Create Human-Centered Products and Services, Kim Goodwin, Alan Cooper

The Inmates are Running the Asylum: Why High Tech Products Drive Us Crazy and How to Restore the Sanity, Alan Cooper

About Face 3: The Essentials of Interaction Design, Alan Cooper, Robert Reimann, David Cronin

The User Is Always Right: A Practical Guide to Creating and Using Personas for the Web, Steve Mulder and Ziv Yaar

The Persona Lifecycle: Keeping People in Mind Throughout Product Design, John Pruitt and Tamara Adlin

6

Ideation and Design Principles

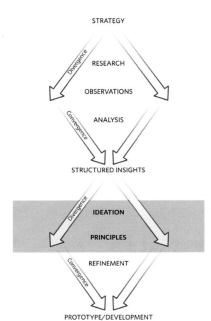

STRATEGY

Divergence

RESEARCH

OBSERVATIONS

Convergence

ANALYSIS

STRUCTURED INSIGHTS

Divergence

IDEATION

PRINCIPLES

Convergence

REFINEMENT

PROTOTYPE/DEVELOPMENT

You know what needs to be designed. You've listened to your business stakeholders and to your users. You've made models of the strategy and of the design research. And now you are staring at a blank piece of paper or screen. You have to, well, design *something*. This is where ideation has to happen.

And once you've come up with tons of ideas, how do you choose which ones are worth pursuing? You use a set of design principles that will not only help select the best ideas, but guide the design through refinement, prototyping, development, and beyond.

But first, let's diverge and come up with concepts.

Creating Concepts

The purpose of brainstorming is not to find the one perfect design for your project. That will come later. Instead, the reason to ideate is to generate many concepts as rapidly as possible. At this point in the design process, quantity — not quality — is what matters the most. You want a wide variety of concepts that approach the project from a wide variety of angles. Even ideas that seem outlandish and completely unfeasible are welcome, because from them, something feasible might evolve (see **Figure 6.1**).

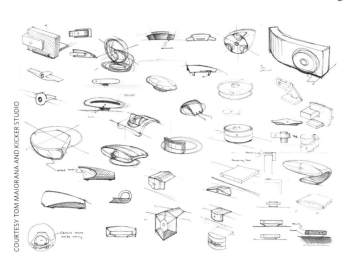

COURTESY TOM MAIORANA AND KICKER STUDIO

Figure 6.1

In ideation, you should strive for as many concepts as possible in as short a period as possible.

As an ideal, each brainstorming session, even a short one of an hour, should generate dozens of ideas. For a new product, you should brainstorm over several days to generate hundreds of ideas, concepts, and fragments of ideas. It doesn't matter if they are variations on an idea, or even if you or others have thought of them before. Just put them down and move on to the next idea.

What you want to do is get every idea you can possibly come up with out there, on paper *as a sketch* not in words (although sometimes giving your concept a name is helpful later, as are words to explain a part of the sketch) so that they can be considered *later*. Be as specific as you can be. No "Fix the thing with a drop down" type notes. Draw the solution you've come up with. The quality of the drawing doesn't matter.

Brainstorming requires some tools. First, because of the limitations of today's available technology, brainstorming should never be done digitally; it should be done with paper, pencils, pens, markers, and possibly white-boards and sticky notes. You need to be able to jot down an idea quickly, set it aside, and move on to the next idea. Fumbling with technology just gets in the way. You can capture your ideas with a digital camera later if necessary. For now, analog means pencil and paper work best.

When brainstorming, designers should have all the research and models close at hand and in view (taped to walls perhaps) for reference and inspira-tion. Also, brainstorming doesn't have to be limited to the designers on the team. Inviting stakeholders, developers, engineers, and even outsiders can sometimes lead to productive ideas you might not have thought of. Just be sure they understand the "rules" of brainstorming:

> ▶ **There are no bad ideas.** There is no judgment about anyone else's ideas.

> ▶ **Stay focused.** Put stray thoughts or unrelated ideas into a "parking lot": a physical place in the room where those sorts of wayward ideas can be captured, but not discussed.

> ▶ **Don't spend a lot of time on any one idea.** In the initial brainstorm-ing sessions especially, the goal is to generate as many ideas as pos-sible. Save going into depth on any one idea for later. For now, more is, indeed, more.

> ▶ **Use the whole room.** Post things up on walls. Simply seeing all the ideas may generate connections between them or generate new ideas.

> ▶ **No multitasking.** You can't do brainstorming well when you are focused on answering email, IMing, texting, or working on other things. It's a concentrated activity, so all distractions should be removed as much as possible.

Larry Tesler on How to be a Good Interaction Designer

Larry Tesler's resume reads like the history of interaction design. He's worked at Xerox PARC, Apple, Amazon, Yahoo!, and now 23andMe. While at Xerox PARC, he helped develop some of the language of interaction design, including pop-up menus and cut-and-paste editing. His law of the Conservation of Complexity (discussed in Chapter 7) is known to programmers and designers alike.

You've worked at some of the seminal places for interaction design: Xerox PARC, Apple, and Amazon. What do they all have in common?

All of them place a high value on both advanced technology and customer delight.

What personal qualities do you think make a good interaction designer?

Enough confidence to believe you can solve any design problem and enough humility to understand that most of your initial ideas are probably bad. Enough humility to listen to ideas from other people that may be better than your own and enough confidence to understand that going with other people's ideas does not diminish your value as a designer.

True concern for the comfort and happiness of other people, including your users and your teammates. If you're not teammate friendly, your products won't be user friendly. That does not mean you should cave in under pressure on an important issue when you have data that supports your opinion. But it does mean you should judge success by the success of the product and the team, not just by the success of your own narrow contribution.

There are a lot of other desirable personal qualities for a designer, such as attention to detail, objectivity, appreciation of humor, appreciation of esthetics, and appreciation of data about users and usage.

What are the most common mistakes that beginning interaction designers make?

What mistakes beginners make varies a lot, partly based on their background and training.

Larry Tesler on How to be a Good Interaction Designer *(continued)*

Some educators, particularly in computer science departments, tell their students to design for themselves as the users. If taken literally, that advice leads to interfaces that only computer science students can use.

I do believe that if you learn to place yourself in the shoes of the user, you can design "for yourself" and really be designing for the user. I call this approach "Method Design" because the mindset is similar to that of Stanislavsky's "method acting." You're really not designing for yourself at all. You're designing for "your character." Of course, to be a successful Method Designer, you need to know your character. That's one reason designers should observe ethnographic studies and usability studies.

Beginners often succumb to pressure from management to "save money" by skipping usability tests despite serious open questions. At the other extreme, beginners sometimes run many more tests than necessary, bring in too many subjects, spend too much time preparing formal reports, or fail to pick their battles.

Usability testing should always be done before a designer finalizes unproven or controversial interface elements. But testing should be conducted in the cheapest possible way. Of course, it is sometimes necessary to demonstrate the value of research to skeptics. In that case, it is worth taking a couple of hours to edit a highlight video showing the severity of the users' confusion.

Two other mistakes made more by beginners than experienced designers are to ignore standards and to follow standards unthinkingly. Consistency is usually good, so you need a really good reason to diverge from standards. But you can not be sure you have a really good reason unless you actually see your users do much better with the custom design element than with the standard.

Choice of words is important. Shorter is usually better. But if you have to explain what "x" means to many of your users—or worse, to your teammates—then you should probably replace "x" by whatever you said to explain it.

Larry Tesler on How to be a Good Interaction Designer *(continued)*

To my mind, what most separates an expert from a beginning designer is the ability to draw from a larger space of potential solutions. Given a particular problem, the beginner and the expert may at first think of the same solution, say, a multi-page flow with numerous forms. But the beginner is likely to fixate on the solution even if it is inordinately complicated. The senior designer will consider radical alternatives, say, a way for the user to see the data as it would look in its final state and edit it in place.

The senior designer won't stop simplifying until the design is simple enough. It need not take months to go through this simplification process. It can take just days, or hours, even seconds. Great design often takes time, but it's wasteful to spend time on approaches that are not simple enough to have a chance of being final.

Are there any unbreakable "laws" in interaction design?

Just one. Design for the users.

Getting Started

Ideation requires being able to make fast mental leaps and connections, so start with a warm-up exercise to get everyone's brains working. For instance, first dwell on the subject at hand in the broadest possible sense. For example, on a project to build an installation for a museum, spend 10 minutes doing a word association game on what art is or what a museum is. Or do drawings based on famous artists. Or have all the people in the room talk about their best (or worst) experience at a museum. What the exercise is doesn't much matter: the point of the warm-up is to get brains, hands, and mouths engaged before starting to generate ideas (see **Figure 6.2**).

Set aside a fixed amount of time for brainstorming—usually not more than two hours at any given time period. Allow for breaks between sessions. It's tiring work and without breaks, it quickly becomes frustrating and tedious. It's also ideal to spread brainstorming over several days. The unconscious will work on the problem while you are sleeping, in the shower, walking, etc. and possibly provide you with concepts and ideas slowly over time.

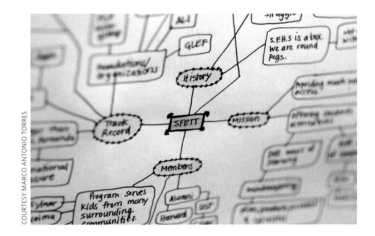

Figure 6.2

Mind maps can be used as a warm-up exercise or for exploring the general subject area. Start with a single word or concept, then branch out from there.

At this point in the design process, no idea is a bad one. Set aside most of what you know about the technical, user, or business constraints (you'll add them back in later). Right now, you want to ask yourself the question Alan Cooper challenges interaction designers to ask: How would it work if it was magic?[1] Meaning, if all the constraints were gone and the user could just push a button, what would happen? How would the system accomplish the task? What would the feedback (see Chapter 7) be like?

Structured Brainstorming

Alan Cooper's "magic" framing is just an example of structured brainstorming. If you've ever sat down to do anything creative, you know that one of the hardest things is to begin. Without any structure, it is easy to stall after one or two ideas or simply stare at a blank page.

Some common structures to use in brainstorming sessions are:

▶ **Pain Points.** Hopefully one of the things learned in design research was what part of the process or activity is problematic or difficult. These moments make excellent focus points to brainstorm around.

▶ **Opportunities.** Likewise, if there are known places for innovation, those can be points to begin.

---

1 Stated in his book *The Inmates are Running the Asylum*

▶   **Process Moments.** If there are known steps in the activity, you can ideate around each of them. Of course, you will eventually have to put the pieces together, but each piece can suggest a greater whole, a framework (see Chapter 7).

▶   **Personas.** Personas generated by design research can also serve as structure by focusing solely on addressing the direct expectations, motivations, and behaviors of one particular persona. Do this for each persona in turn.

▶   **Metaphors.** Human brains work in metaphors.[2] We can harness this natural ability to compare unlike objects to aid brainstorming. Sometimes by using metaphor, you can discover a framework that can wrap around the whole project. What is this product like? What is the product not like? For example, what if you thought of a mobile device as a toy? As a musical instrument? As a cooking utensil? Sometimes, the oddest metaphors will uncover a previously unthought-of direction for the design.

Spend a fixed amount of time (30-60 minutes) on each pain point, opportunity, process moment, etc., then take a break. Then move on to the next session (see **Figure 6.3**).

Figure 6.3

Ideation around a single screen, showing various layouts. Tracing paper was laid over the previous iteration and then sketched on.

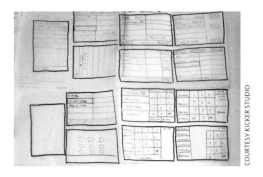

COURTESY KICKER STUDIO

There are many other known brainstorming techniques[3] that can help structure your ideation sessions.

2 See the great book *Metaphors We Live By,* by George Lakoff and Mark Johnson
3 For an amazingly complete list, see All Known Idea Generation Methods, compiled by Jack Martin Leith at http://www.jackmartinleith.com/idea-generation-methods/

Here are samples that are especially good for interaction designers:

▶   **Brainwriting.** Each person writes down or sketches the beginning of an idea silently on a piece of paper. This could be as simple as a single word or a shape. After three minutes, the person passes the paper to his neighbor, who continues the idea. This repeats around the circle until it gets all the way back around to its originator.

▶   **Break the Rules.** Rather than ignore the constraints you (hopefully by now) understand, you list them and one-by-one figure out how to break them.

▶   **Force Fit.** Distill the problem down to two words that are in opposition, then put those words together into a phrase. For example, "intense peace." Ruminate on what exists in the world that embodies that phrase, then try to apply it to the project for inspiration. Nature and art often work well for this.

▶   **Poetry.** Reduce the problem down to a haiku or short poem. Such a small form makes you figure out what is most important.

▶   **Questioning.** Start with a very general concept and keep asking two questions: how and why. For example, "We are going to build a social networking site." Why? "So record collectors can exchange albums." How? "By uploading their rare albums." How? Etc.

▶   **Laddering.** Laddering means either moving "up" to a level of abstraction ("What is this problem an example of?") or moving "down" to something concrete ("What is an example of this problem?"). Laddering is especially good for getting unstuck.

▶   **Swiping.** Swiping means stealing the best ideas from another field or domain. It starts by abstracting your problem ("This is about finding something small") and asking what other products or fields have ways of doing the abstraction.

▶   **Bizarro World.** Pretend you wanted to make the opposite product or the opposite outcome. Invert everything: what is good is bad, what is desirable isn't, etc.

It's not a bad idea to incentivize idea generation as well. Small rewards or prizes for the most ideas generated, or a group reward once you reach 100 concepts, can do wonders for enthusiasm. To be more egalitarian, give everyone a raffle ticket for each concept generated, then pick a prizewinner at the end of a session.

Organizing Concepts

Once you've generated your concepts, it's a good idea to spend some time organizing them. Just like with data generated via design research, it's good to cluster, name, and sort all the ideas you've created so that it is easy to examine and discuss them (see **Figure 6.4**).

Figure 6.4

Concepts clustered by activity around managing diabetes.

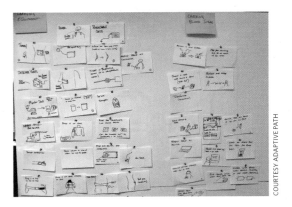

COURTESY ADAPTIVE PATH

Give each idea a number, or better yet, a descriptive name, especially for major concepts. Collapse similar concepts together, as there will likely be duplicate ideas.

As a way of comparing concepts, it might make sense to sort them by various criteria. You can put them on a 2×2 matrix (see Chapter 5) to show where each falls on a continuum. You can put them into a spreadsheet, labeled by attribute ("safe," "powerful," etc.).

The purpose of organizing concepts is so that when you have your design principles, it is easy to use them as a lens on the ideas you've already generated.

Creating Design Principles

Once you have your concepts, how do you determine which ones are worth pursuing? That's where design principles come in.

Design principles are a set of phrases designed to help guide design decisions throughout the remainder of the design process—and even beyond, after the product launches. They can be thought of almost as design requirements, except they should not be a specific prescription for solving a particular problem; rather, they are general statements that apply across the project. Think of them as a design strategy, the same way there is a business strategy.

Let's say, for example, you are designing a new recipe display for kitchens and you've noticed people's hands can get covered in flour or other foodstuffs while cooking—too soiled to be able to operate most controls easily. Thus, one of your design principles might be Operate with Messy Hands. It's almost a requirement, but it applies across a number of features and suggests the concepts that might work well for the product, such as touchscreens, voice commands, or maybe a gestural interface. Using this principle would also stop you from designing small buttons or using materials that couldn't be cleaned easily. And it might also cause you to discard many of the concepts you came up with during ideation.

Design principles are a combination of three things:

▸ What is known about the users, the context of use, and the design strategy.

▸ The best ideas/themes that emerged from ideation sessions.

▸ What the designer thinks is necessary for a successful project, based on experience or subject matter expertise.

Using our recipe display example, other design principles might be Help From Across the Room, Allow for Improvisation, and Act Like a Sous Chef.

The best design principles are:

▸ **Pithy.** A short phrase is best. If it needs to be described, you can do that, but make sure it has a short phrase as a lead-in because you want it to be…

▸ **Memorable.** The best design principles can be remembered easily by everyone on the team. Funny, witty, and provocative statements and plays on words work best.

▸ **Cross-feature.** Design principles should be applicable across the product. If you can't apply it to more than one feature, it's probably a requirement, not a principle.

▸ **Specific.** Easy to Use is not a design principle. It is too general, and doesn't give any guidance on making a decision between options while refining (see Chapter 7). Of course it should be easy to use (and intuitive, and delightful, and innovative, and other clichés) but what about this particular product is unique?

▸ **A differentiator.** After you've made your design principles, see if they as a whole could be applied to a competitor (if there is one). If they can, then they probably aren't specific enough (or your product isn't differentiated enough).

▸ **Non-conflicting.** You want the product to be harmonious, and you don't want to pit one principle against another, so be careful not to create principles that might be in conflict once applied, such as Never Ask Questions vs. Give The User Total Control.

Case Study: TiVo

The Company

TiVo, the preeminent digital video recorder (DVR) manufacturer.

The Problem

In the late 1990s, no one had a DVR—because they didn't exist yet. TiVo had the problem of how to design and launch a technology that was incredibly disruptive to how people were used to watching TV, but make it so that it was understandable, accessible, and fit into people's lives and, especially, living rooms.

The Process

The TiVo team created a set of principles (they called them "tenents"), some of which are still in use a decade and several versions of the device later. The mantras were:

▸   It's entertainment, stupid.

▸   It's TV, stupid.

▸   It's video, dammit.

▸   Everything is smooth and gentle.

▸   No modality or deep hierarchy.

▸   Respect the viewer's privacy.

▸   It's a robust appliance, like a TV.

Case Study: TiVo *(continued)*

The reason the TiVo creators made these principles was not only to help guide the experience of using TiVo, but also to remind the internal team not to think about the TiVo device as a computer (which it essentially is—a large hard drive and the Linux operating system). Users weren't going to use it like a computer—they were going to be on their sofa, 10 feet away from the screen, wanting to be entertained and not wanting to make a lot of choices. Since it was a new technology, its adoption depended on its design to demonstrate its value.

The Solution

There is little doubt that TiVo changed the nature of television. Dozens of accolades and even Emmys for their product have followed in the decade since the service was initially launched. Some of this is clearly due to the adherence to the set of design tenents, which even today differentiate them from their competitors. TiVo is still frequently listed on the Best Products of the Year awards.

Once you have your design principles, you can use them as a measuring stick against the concepts you've generated to see which ones best fit. Hopefully several ideas will work within the guidelines, or could be tinkered with to fit.

But design principles can also be used from this point in the process forward to help make design decisions. When there are multiple options to choose from ("Should we ask users first, or just do it for them?"), the design principles can sometimes help make the correct decision clear.

Design principles can sometimes outlast the specific product itself, or even be extended across lines of products to give them all a similar grounding.

Summary

Brainstorming can be mysterious. Frequently an idea will come to you when you are not in a brainstorming session. Ideas seem to have a life of their own, but they can sometimes be coaxed into existence, and that's what you hope ideation will do.

The design principles you create are a way—granted, a subjective way—of measuring your ideas for value and feasibility. Of course, the only way to really tell if an idea is a good one is to play with it, test it out, and refine it. That is the topic of the next chapter.

For Further Reading

Six Thinking Hats, Edward de Bono

A Technique for Producing Ideas, James Webb Young

Thinkertoys: A Handbook of Creative-Thinking Techniques, Michael Michalko

The Seeds of Innovation: Cultivating the Synergy That Fosters New Ideas, Elaine Dundon

7

Refinement

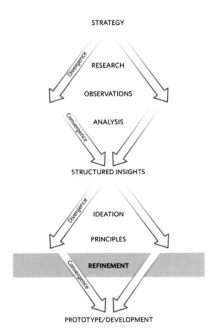

Having a concept, no matter how brilliant, is not enough for a product. Concepts are relatively easy to come by; it is the execution of those concepts that matters. And execution is all about defining the details of the concept, fleshing it out until it works in a functionally- and aesthetically-pleasing way. Execution means refining the concept in order to work on the **details**.

Details are the small parts of the design where designers earn their paychecks. They provide moments of efficiency and delight for users, and are also where designers earn the respect of the developers, businesspeople, and manufacturers. Details often get overlooked in just concept projects. Constraints also are somehow less solid in the world of concepting than they are once you start to figure out how the product actually works.

Constraints

It's at this point in the process where constraints really rear their ugly head. Hopefully, via stakeholder interviews and design research (and experience), you're aware of a number of constraints by now:

▸ **Time.** How much time do you have to finish the project? When does the product need to launch/ship?

▸ **Money.** What's the budget for finishing the project? What's the price point or the business model of the product?

▸ **Technology.** What platform is the solution going to be made on? What systems are or need to be in place for this to work? Can you have the technology you need in the given time and budget?

▸ **Business needs.** How will this meet the business success metrics? What organizational support is there for this product?

▸ **User needs.** What does the user need to accomplish? How will this be better than any other solution? Does the solution have to be accessible to those with disabilities?

▸ **Context.** Are there physical limitations of size or weight? Where will the product be used, and how does that affect it?

> ▶ **Tools.** What kind of tools (software, manufacturing) will be used to build and maintain the product?

> ▶ **Teams.** What kind of team do you have to build this? What are their skills? Realistically, what can you collectively accomplish in the time given?

> ▶ **You.** What skills do you have? What are your weaknesses, and how can they be overcome?

Constraints end up defining the product more than one cares to admit. The best designers are those who can juggle the most constraints. "Design depends largely on constraints," noted Charles Eames. The trick is to figure out which constraints are impossible barriers and which can be moved or changed, given enough effort.

All projects, no matter what their constraints, should follow certain general principles and fundamentals of interaction design.

The Laws and Principles of Interaction Design

Interaction design, being a new field, doesn't have very many hard and fast rules, or "laws," to speak of. In a sense, interaction designers are still figuring out many of the basic principles of the work they do. However, there is a handful of laws that interaction designers may use from time to time, as well as basic principles that underlie all interaction design work. These laws and principles should always guide the work, not dictate it.

Direct and Indirect Manipulation

Objects can be manipulated in two ways: directly and indirectly. Although technically digital objects can be manipulated only indirectly (you can't touch something that's made of bits and bytes, after all), direct and indirect manipulation represent two ways of thinking about how to work with objects.

Direct manipulation is a term coined by University of Maryland professor Ben Shneiderman in the early 1980s. It refers to the process in which, by selecting a digital object with a finger or with a mouse or with some other extension of the hand, we can then do something to the object: move it, turn it, drag it to the trash, change its color, and so on. We can mimic an action that we might perform on a similar object in the physical world. For example, we can scale an object by dragging a corner of it as though we were stretching it. Direct manipulation, because it more closely maps to our physical experiences, is supposedly more easily learned and used, especially for manipulating 3-D objects in digital space.

Of course, we also directly manipulate physical objects all the time, by pushing buttons, turning dials, flipping switches, and so on, which can cause either mechanical or digital effects. Through sensors, the behavior of objects can be affected by movement, such as an MP3 player with an accelerometer going into shuffle mode by being shaken.

In **indirect manipulation**, we use a command or menu or gesture in space or voice command that isn't directly a part of the digital object to alter that object. Choosing the Select All command in a menu and pressing the Delete key on the keyboard are examples of indirect manipulation. In the past, especially during the years before the Macintosh popularized the GUI, nearly all computer commands were indirect.

Interaction designers need to decide how digital objects in their products can be manipulated: directly, indirectly, or (more and more frequently) in both ways.

Figure 7.1

The design of this gate latch provides visual affordances indicating how it should be used.

Affordances

How something manifests gives us cues as to how it behaves and how we should interact with it (**Figure 7.1**). The size, shape, and even weight of mobile devices let us know that they should be carried with us. The sleek black or silver look of digital video recorders like TiVo devices tell us that they are pieces of electronic equipment and belong alongside stereos and televisions.

Appearance is the major source of what cognitive psychologist James Gibson, in 1966, called *affordances*. Gibson explored the concept more fully in his 1979 book *The Ecological Approach to Visual Perception,* but it wasn't until Don Norman's seminal book *The Psychology of Everyday Things*, in 1988, that the term spread into design. An affordance is a property, or set of properties, that provides some indication of how to interact with an object or feature. A chair has an affordance of sitting because of its shape. A button has an affordance of pushing because of its shape and the way it moves (or seemingly moves). The empty space in a cup is an affordance that tells us we could fill the cup with liquid. An affordance (or, technically, a *perceived* affordance) is contextual and cultural. You know you can push a button because you've pushed one before. On the other hand, a person who has never seen chopsticks would be puzzled about what to do with them.

Interaction design, especially in the refinement phase, can be thought of in part as providing affordances so that the features and functionality of a product can be discovered and correctly used.

Feedback and Feedforward

Feedback, as the term is commonly used in interaction design, is some indication that something has happened. Feedback should occur like crooked voting: early and often. Every action by a person who engages with the product or service, no matter how slightly, should be accompanied by some acknowledgment of the action: Moving the mouse should move the cursor. Pressing a key on your mobile phone should display a number.

To proceed otherwise is to court errors, some of them potentially serious. Frequently, if there is no immediate or obvious feedback, users will repeat the action they just did—for instance, pushing a button twice. Needless to say, this can cause problems, such as accidentally buying an item twice or transferring money multiple times. If the button is connected to dangerous machinery, it could result in injury or death. People need feedback.

Designing the *appropriate* feedback is the designer's task. The designer has to determine how quickly the product or service will respond and in what manner. Should the response be something simple such as the appearance of a letter on a screen (the feedback in word processing for pressing a key), or should it be a complex indicator such as a pattern of blinking LED lights on a device that monitors your stock portfolio?

There is little more annoying than talking to someone who doesn't respond. The same holds true for "conversations" with products and services. We need to know that the product "heard" what we told it to do and that it is working on that task. We also want to know what the product or service is doing. A spinning circle or a tiny hourglass icon doesn't give users much transparency into what is happening.

Figure 7.2

The Orbitz searching screen won't make the wait shorter for search results, but it will make it seem shorter because of its responsiveness.

If a response to an action is going to take significant time (more than 1 second, which, believe it or not, can seem like a long wait), a good design provides some mechanism that lets the user know the system has heard the request and is doing something (**Figure 7.2**). This doesn't shorten the waiting time, but it makes it seem shorter. Excellent examples of such a mechanism are the indicators that tell you how long software installation will take. These indicators also assure the user that the process hasn't stalled.

The responsiveness of digital products, determined by the time between an action and the product's response (also called **latency**), can be characterized by these four basic levels:

> ▷ **Immediate.** When a product or service responds in 0.1 second or less, the user considers the response immediate and continues the task with no perceived interruption. When you push a key on your keyboard and a letter instantly appears, that is an immediate response.

> ▷ **Stammer.** If a product or service takes 0.1 second to 1 second to respond, users will notice a delay. If such a delay is not frequently repeated, users will overlook it. Repeated, it will make the product or service feel sluggish. For instance, if you press a key on your keyboard and it takes a second for the letter to appear on your screen, you'll notice the delay. If this happens with every key press, you will quickly become frustrated with your word processor.

> ▷ **Interruption.** After a second of no response, users will feel that the task they were doing was interrupted and their focus will shift from the task at hand to the product or service itself. If you click a Submit button to execute a stock trade and nothing happens for several seconds, you will worry about the trade and wonder if the Web site is broken. Multiple interruptions can lead to a disruption.

▶ **Disruption.** If a delay of more than 10 seconds occurs, users will consider the task at hand completely disrupted. Feedback such as a progress bar or a timer that indicates how long a process will take will allay users' concerns and also allow the user to decide whether to continue the process. Marquees in the London Underground indicating when the next trains will arrive are excellent examples of responsiveness that addresses this level of delay.

Related to feedback and also to affordance is what designer Tom Djajadiningrat calls **feedforward**: knowing what will happen *before* you perform an action. Feedforward can be a straightforward message ("Pushing this button will submit your order") or simple cues such as hypertext links with descriptive names instead of "Here."

Feedforward allows users to perform an action with confidence because it gives them an idea of what will happen next. It is harder to design into products and services than feedback, but designers should keep an eye out for opportunities to use it.

Mental Model

Mental model is the term for a user's internal understanding of how a system or object works, which may or may not reflect how the thing actually does work. The best mental models allow for a deep understanding of the thing, minus the complexities involved in making the thing work. For instance, most people have a mental model of how a car behaves, even though they don't know how a combustion engine works.

Mental models are usually constructed by users from the cues provided by the designer in the form of affordances, feedback, and feedforward. Indeed, using those very things, designers can manipulate the user's mental model significantly, hiding or exposing the product's inner workings. For example, a label on a car's steering wheel that reads, "Blow horn before starting car" would certainly change how you think about the functionality of the car, and especially the horn. Or imagine if when you turned the car on, a voice instructed the driver about fuel going into the engine. Sure, you would know more about the car, but it wouldn't make your driving any better.

Standards

There is a perennial debate among interaction designers about how closely to follow interface standards and when to break them. Do all applications have to work in a similar way? Should Ctrl-C or Command-C always copy whatever is selected? Does every menu bar have to have the same headings (File, Edit, View, and so on)? Both Microsoft and Apple have standards guidelines online that are religiously followed by many. Usability gurus such as Jakob Nielsen promote and swear by them.

There are certainly good reasons for having and using standards. Over many years, designers have trained users to expect certain items to be located in certain places (for example, the company logo goes at the top left of a Web site) and certain features to work in a particular way (for example, pressing Ctrl-Z undoes the last command). A design that ignores these conventions means that your users will have to learn something different, something that doesn't work like all their other applications work. A variation from the standard can cause frustration and annoyance.

So why ever violate or alter standards? Alan Cooper solved this dilemma with his axiom: *Obey standards unless there is a truly superior alternative.* That is, ignore standards only when the new way of doing a task is markedly, significantly better than what the users have previously used. Feel free to propose a new method of cutting and pasting, but it had better be unequivocally better than what users are accustomed to now. New standards don't have to be radical departures from the old standards, but even a slight change should be made with care because it subverts the user's expectations of how a product should work.

Fitts's Law

Published in 1954 by psychologist Paul Fitts, Fitts's (pronounced "fitzez") Law simply states that the time it takes to move from a starting position to a final target is determined by two things: the distance to the target and the size of the target. Fitts's Law models the act of pointing, both with a finger and with a device like a mouse. The larger the target, the faster it can be pointed to. Likewise, the closer the target, the faster it can be pointed to.

Fitts's Law has three main implications for interaction designers. Since the size of the target matters, clickable objects like buttons need to be a reasonable size. This is especially true for touchscreens or on screens at a distance such as a television. As anyone who has tried to click a tiny icon will attest, the smaller the object, the harder it is to select. Second, the edges and corners of screens are excellent places to position things like menu bars and buttons. Edges and corners are huge targets because they basically have infinite height or width. You can't overshoot them with the mouse; your mouse will stop on the edge of the screen no matter how far you move it, and thus will land on top of the button or menu. The third major implication of Fitts's Law is that controls that appear next to what the user is working on (such as a menu that appears next to an object when the user right-clicks the mouse) can usually be opened more quickly than pull-down menus or toolbars, which require travel to other parts of the screen.

Hick's Law

Hick's Law, or the Hick-Hyman Law, says that the time it takes for users to make decisions is determined by the number of possible choices they have. People don't consider a group of possible choices one by one. Instead, they subdivide the choices into categories, eliminating about half of the remaining choices with each step in the decision. Thus, Hick's Law claims that a user will more quickly make choices from one menu of 10 items than from two menus of 5 items each.

A controversial implication of this law is that it is better for products to give users many choices simultaneously instead of organizing the choices into hierarchical groups, as in drop-down menus. If followed to an extreme, this approach could create some truly frightening designs. Imagine if a content-rich site like Yahoo or Amazon presented all of its links on the home page, or if your mobile phone displayed all of its features on its main screen.

Hick's Law also states that the time it takes to make a decision is affected by two factors: familiarity with the choices, such as from repeated use, and the format of the choices—are they sounds or words, videos, or buttons?

The Magical Number Seven

Hick's Law seems to run counter to George Miller's Magical Number Seven rule. In 1956, Miller, a Princeton University psychology professor, determined that the human mind is best able to remember information in chunks of seven items, "plus or minus two."[1] After five to nine pieces of information (for instance, navigation labels or a list of features or a set of numbers), the human mind starts making errors. It seems that we have difficulty keeping more than that amount of information in our short-term memory at any given time.

Some designers have taken the Magical Number Seven rule to an extreme, making sure that there are never any more than seven items on a screen at any given time. This is a bit excessive, because Miller was specifically talking about bits of information that humans have to remember or visualize in short-term memory. When those bits of information are displayed on a screen, users don't have to keep them in their short-term memory; they can always refer to them.

But designers should take care not to design a product that causes "cognitive overload" by ignoring the Magical Number Seven rule. For example, designers should never create a device that forces users to remember unfamiliar items across screens or pages. Imagine if you had to type a new phone number on three separate screens of your mobile phone. You'd scramble to do so before the number faded from your short-term memory.

Tesler's Law of the Conservation of Complexity

Larry Tesler, one of the pioneers of interaction design (see the interview with him in Chapter 6), coined Tesler's Law of the Conservation of Complexity, which states that some complexity is inherent in every process. There is a point beyond which you can't simplify the process any further; you can only move the inherent complexity from one place to another.

For example, for an e-mail message, two elements are required: your e-mail address and the address of the person to whom you are sending the mail. If either of these items is missing, the e-mail can't be sent, and your e-mail client will tell you so. It's a necessary complexity. But some of that burden has likely been shifted to your e-mail client. You don't typically have to enter your e-mail address every time you send e-mail. The e-mail program handles that task for you. Likewise, the e-mail client probably also helps you by remembering e-mail addresses to which you've sent mail in the past, so that you don't

---

1   See "The magical number seven, plus or minus two: Some limits on our capacity for processing information" Psychological Review, 63, 81-97

have to remember them and type them in fully each time. The complexity isn't gone, though—instead, some of it has been shifted to the software.

Interaction designers need to be aware of Tesler's Law for two reasons. First, designers need to acknowledge that all processes have elements that cannot be made simpler, no matter how much they tinker with them. Second, designers need to look for reasonable places to move this complexity in the products they make. It doesn't make sense for users to type their e-mail addresses in every e-mail they send when the software can handle this task. The burden of complexity needs to be shared as much as possible by the products interaction designers make.

The Poka-Yoke Principle

Legendary Japanese industrial engineer and quality guru Shigeo Shingo created the Poka-Yoke Principle in 1961 while working for Toyota. Poka-Yoke roughly translates in English to mistake proofing: avoiding (**yokeru**) inadvertent errors (**poka**). Designers use Poka-Yoke when they put constraints on products to prevent errors, forcing users to adjust their behavior and correctly execute an operation.

Simple examples of the application of Poka-Yoke are the cords (USB, FireWire, power, and others) that fit into electronic devices only in a particular way and in a particular place, and thus prevent someone from, say, plugging the power cord into the hole where the headphones go (**Figure 7.3**). In this way, Poka-Yoke ensures that proper conditions exist *before* a process begins, preventing problems from occurring in the first place. Poka-Yoke can be implemented in lots of forms: by signs (Do not touch the third rail!), procedures (Step 1: Unplug toaster), humans (police directing traffic around an accident), or any other entity that prevents incorrect execution of a process step. Where prevention is not possible, Poka-Yoke mandates that problems be stopped as early as possible in the process.

Figure 7.3

An illustration of the Poka-Yoke Principle. The USB cord will fit into only a particular slot on this laptop computer.

Poka-Yoke often manifests itself in interaction design via the disabling of functionality (or the navigation, for example, the menu item or the icon) when conditions for its use have not yet been met. When doing this, it's also a good practice when possible to show via tool tip or other means what conditions will enable the functionality.

Errors

In an ideal situation, no system should ever present an error message to a user unless the user has done everything *right* but the system itself cannot respond correctly. "Errors" are often a sign of poor design or engineering, or of not applying the Poka-Yoke Principle.

When an error occurs, you should always provide a way to fix the error, or otherwise provide information about why the error occurred.

Frameworks

Every product needs a framework: an actual or metaphysical structure that defines the product and integrates the content and functionality into a unified whole. Without it, your product will seem disjointed, a collection of random stuff that users will struggle to make sense of.

There are three main kinds of frameworks that can be applied to a product: metaphor, postures, and structure.

Metaphor

Metaphor can be a way for users to understand abstract (digital) concepts. The most famous example, of course, is the desktop metaphor, which helped unify the graphical user interface (GUI) we've used for the last 30 years. Metaphor can suggest everything from how a product should function to how its visual or physical form is shaped.

Of course, metaphor can be abused. Witness Microsoft's infamous Bob (**Figure 7.4**), which imagined the operating system as a physical house. And metaphor can also be inaccurate—you can't do everything on your virtual desktop that you can on your physical one, after all. But it can be a powerful frameworking tool.

COURTESY MICROSOFT

Figure 7.4

Microsoft's Bob is an
example of metaphor
run amok.

Dashboards and Control Panels

A very common metaphor is that of a dashboard or control panel (**Figure 7.5**). Many of the applications, Web sites, consumer electronics, and appliances use this metaphor, lifted directly from physical objects, as a way of clustering and grouping both system information and controls.

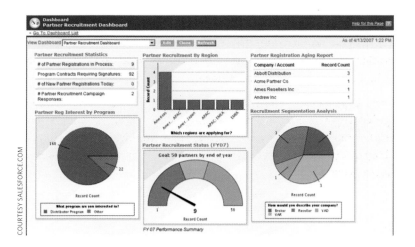

COURTESY SALESFORCE.COM

Figure 7.5

An example of a
dashboard-style
layout.

Postures

Over the last 30 years, several common types of structures have emerged for the design of software. Alan Cooper calls these **postures**[2] and there are four principal ones:

- ▸ **Sovereign.** For applications users will need to use often, intensively, and for long periods of time, a sovereign posture might make sense. Sovereign applications such as Microsoft Word are complex, large, and take up a large portion of the screen when in use. Sovereign applications have many features and lots of work or viewing space, and typically the application window is broken up into several panes (for example, one pane for an overview, one for working, one for a detail view).

- ▸ **Transient.** For applications that are temporary and users need only briefly, such as installers and widgets like calculators, transient posture is appropriate. Transient applications use only a small amount of screen real estate and have few, simple controls that are clearly labeled.

- ▸ **Daemonic.** Applications that mostly run in the background, such as Growl or virus detectors, often utilize the daemonic posture. Unless absolutely necessary, these applications shouldn't intrude on the user's attention. The controls for them are mostly limited to setup and configuration through a simple control panel.

- ▸ **Parasitic.** An application, such as the Windows Start bar or Tweet-Deck, that supplements another application or service can have a parasitic posture. Parasitic posture applications are present for long periods, but are generally smaller than sovereign applications and have limited functionality.

Structure

Even if you choose a posture such as sovereign, you will likely have to determine, at least roughly, what overall form and layout it will take, such as the layout of panes in the application. And if there is particular hardware involved, such as on a mobile device or piece of consumer electronics, the interplay between hardware and software has to be considered as well.

---

2 For more details on postures, see *About Face 3.0*

Functional Cartography

If your project combines hardware and software, you need to determine where the functionality "lives." This is the **functional cartography**. Once you have a list of functionality and an understanding of their context of use, you can go about determining whether the controls for that functionality should be analog (physical buttons, sliders, dials, and so on), digital (onscreen controls), or some hybrid of the two (for example, soft keys). Soft keys are physical buttons alongside screen labels, and the context changes the functionality (and accompanying label) of the button.

How the functional cartography is decided depends on a number of factors:

▸   **Context.** When and where will the functionality be used? Does it need to be accessed rapidly? In the dark or unseen (in a pocket or behind the device)? With the screen idle or off?

▸   **Priority.** How important is this piece of functionality? Does it always need to be available? Is it used very often?

▸   **Cost.** How much does it cost (in terms of money, resources, weight, and power consumption) to have a screen at all? Or an additional physical control?

▸   **Ergonomics.** For the target users, what is the easiest physically to use?

▸   **Aesthetics.** Is another physical control going to ruin the form? Is the screen needed to have these controls going to be too large?

▸   **Tangibility.** How tactile does the feature need to be? Does it need to have the presence (and resulting affordance) of a physical control, or does a touchscreen (perhaps with haptic feedback) work as well?

The resulting functional cartography can be documented in a variety of ways. Often a simple table will suffice, with columns for Physical and Digital, and the functionality in rows below, showing in which category they will be placed. Another way to document (if you are farther along in the design process) is an illustration or sketch of the physical form, noting the functionality that resides on- and off-screen.

Once a functional cartography is done, it becomes easier to sketch, model, and prototype the device, as the location of functional pieces is now better known. A functional cartography need not be set in stone, however. During prototyping or modeling, it might become clear that a physical control is necessary, or vice versa. But a functional cartography will at least give a starting place to distribute features and discuss the interplay between form and function.

Site/Screen/State Maps

One way of determining structure organically is to figure out how the pieces of functionality flow into one another and how the user navigates between them. This is often done after a task flow (see later in this chapter) has been made.

On the Web, this is sometimes accomplished via a site map (**Figure 7.6**), as different pieces of functionality live in different physical areas of the site, accessed by hyperlinks. This is also true of other products like mobile phones where, for example, Web browsing is often in a separate space from dialing the phone.

Figure 7.6

A simple site map.

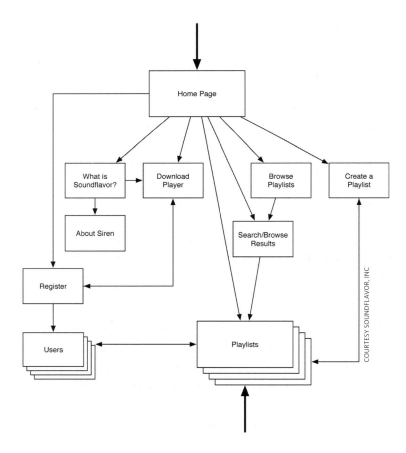

The organization and labeling of features, information, and content is the discipline of **information architecture**. Information architecture draws upon library science techniques to structure information spaces in ways that make finding, navigating between, and understanding content easy.

But increasingly, even on the Web, functionality involves not going to another area, but simply shifting state. Practically every product involving interaction design changes over time. A **state** can be thought of as a paused moment of a time-based system. A state captures a particular moment in an interaction. States to pay particular attention to are initiation, activation, and updates.[3] Initiation is the default state immediately before an action begins. What does the screen (if any) look like, and what does the user do to change that (for example, rolling over a button, clicking a link)? Activation is what happens during an action. For example, what happens while the user is dragging an item across the screen or when a button is pushed? Updates are the state after the user has finished an action, how the product has changed.

Modes are a general condition created by the user or the system that allows for different functionality (and/or different states) to be accessed. For example, in some applications, you can only affect content when you go into editing mode. Modes are controversial in that they add complexity to any system and make mental models more challenging. They also create a lot more *conditional situations* that need to be documented and accounted for. In addition to pages or screens, you can create a flow between modes and states as well.

Mapping out pages, screens, states, and modes can create an overview that helps unify the product for *you*. You still need to pay attention to the overall impression that you're giving your users via affordances and feedback. Users need to understand the product as a whole before becoming familiar with the details.

Documentation and Methods of Refinement

Product concepts are refined mostly by thinking through them, which means either by simply starting to build them (see Chapter 8) or by putting ideas on paper, whiteboard, or screen and seeing where they lead. The

---

3 See *Plans and Situated Actions: The Problem of Human–Machine Communication* by Lucy Suchman

documents generated by this process are typically called documentation, but that implies detailing something that is completed. These are working documents that should evolve over time; documentation is an unfortunate name for them.

Designers should create exactly as much documentation as it takes to execute the project well, and no more. If the designer's team responds well to use cases, then by all means the designer should produce them. If a client couldn't care less about them, the designer shouldn't do one unless the designer or the team finds it helpful.

If a document doesn't communicate anything useful, it is worthless—less than worthless, in fact, because it squanders the designer's time. Each document produced should take the project one step closer to completion.

Scenarios

Scenarios provide a fast and effective way to imagine the design concepts in use. In a sense, scenarios are prototypes built of words.

Scenarios are, at their heart, simply stories—stories about what it will be like to use the product or service once it has been made. The protagonists of these stories are the personas (see chapter 5). Using a scenario, designers can place their personas into context and further bring them to life. Indeed, scenarios are one of the factors that make personas worth having. Running through the same scenario using different personas is an excellent technique for uncovering what needs to be included in the final product.

Consider an e-commerce Web site, for example. One persona is Juan, a very focused shopper who always knows exactly what he wants. Another persona is Angela, who likes to look around and compare items. If the designer imagines them in a scenario in which they are shopping for an item, the scenario starring Juan will have him using search tools, and the scenario starring Angela will have her using browsing tools.

One common scenario that works well for almost every product or service is one that imagines first-time use. What happens when the personas encounter the product or service for the first time? How do they know what to do and how to use the product or service? What does it feel like to them? Running each persona through a first-time use scenario can reveal how to tailor the final design to appeal to and work for each persona.

A picture can be worth a thousand words, but a few words can also be worth quite a few pictures. Consider this example from a scenario for an online grocery delivery service:

Sarah logs onto her BigGrocery account. She sees her order from last week and decides to use it again for this week's order. She removes a few items by dragging them off her BigGroceryList. Her total cost adjusts appropriately. She has all the groceries she wants now, so she clicks the Deliver button. Her saved credit card account is charged, and her confirmation page tells her to expect the groceries in about an hour.

This scenario took only a few minutes to write, but it would have taken hours to storyboard, days to wireframe, and weeks to prototype. Using scenarios, designers can sketch with words.

Sketches and Models

Of course, designers can sketch with images as well as words (**Figure 7.7**). As stated earlier, the designer's best tool has been and continues to be the physical drawing surface (paper, whiteboard) and the physical drawing instrument (pencil, pen, crayon, marker). Nothing digital thus far has been able to match the flexibility, speed, and ease of sketching on a piece of paper or whiteboard. Space is just one reason—even the largest monitor cannot compete with wall-sized whiteboards or sheets of paper fastened together.

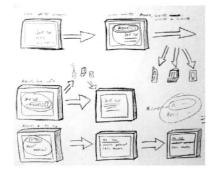

Figure 7.7

Before opening up any software, spend some quality time sketching with pens, pencils, and paper. Sketches have the added bonus of looking unfinished, so no one is inhibited from discussing their flaws.

Another form of sketching is modeling, which is useful for exploring physical forms. Models can be made of a variety of materials, from clay to cardboard to Styrofoam. Large blocks of Styrofoam can even be used to model physical spaces. Even crude blocks of wood, like those carried around by Jeff Hawkins to test the size, shape, and weight of the original PalmPilot,[4]

---

4 See, for instance, "Jeff Hawkins: The Man Who Almost Single-Handedly Revived The Handheld Computer Industry" by Shawn Barnett in *Pen Computing* magazine. Online at www.pencomputing.com/palm/Pen33/hawkins1.html

can be models. Models, like sketches, can be rapidly put together, to give rough approximations of physical objects and environments.

Sketching and modeling should be done throughout the design process, of course, but they are most helpful as visualizations of concepts and ideas that are still being formed to help to clarify and communicate those ideas and concepts.

Sketches and models are, by their nature, informal, and they can be easily changed. Viewers feel free to comment on them for just this very reason. This is a good thing, and no designer should feel overly attached to them.

Storyboards

Once a scenario and sketches have been created to show what a product or service could be like, designers can create a storyboard (**Figure 7.8**) to help illustrate the product or service in use.

Figure 7.8

This storyboard was done with photography, but many storyboards are drawn.

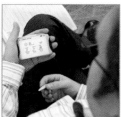

Dave writes the word *Weather* and circles it.

The page is replaced by the local weather forecast.

After reading the page, Dave draws an X across it and the page disappears.

Storyboarding is a technique drawn from filmmaking and advertising. Combining a narrative with accompanying images, designers can powerfully tell a story about a product or service, displaying its features in a context.

The images on a storyboard can be illustrations or staged photos created expressly for the storyboard. Generic or stock images are not recommended, as they will come off as stilted and likely won't be specific enough to match the scenario). Storyboards consist of these image panels, with accompanying text that can be drawn directly from the scenarios.

Storyboards can also be used in conjunction with a wireframe (discussed later in this chapter) to illustrate the details of a complicated process or function. Using a storyboard, a designer can show key moments of an action. For example, a complicated drag-and-drop procedure could be shown with panels illustrating the first moment that the user picks up an object, what happens during dragging, and what happens when the object is dropped.

Task Flows

Once you know what tasks have to be designed for (possibly after doing a task analysis as detailed in Chapter 5), putting those tasks into a sensible order, or flow, is important. Task flows (**Figure 7.9**) show the logical connections that will be built into wireframes (discussed later in this chapter). You can't, for instance, use the Back button on your Web browser to go back to a previous page until you've been to more than one page. You can't connect a phone call until you've entered a number. You can't change your preferences until you've registered. And so on.

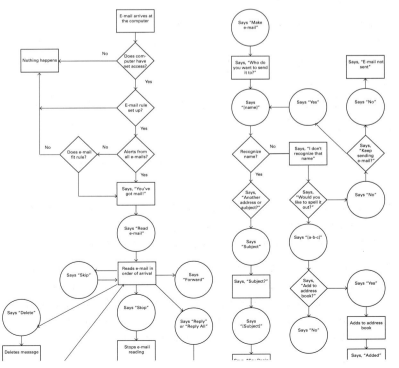

Figure 7.9

A task flow for a voice interface.

Putting tasks into flows helps the designer begin to see the product take shape. Task flows can suggest page order on a Web site or in a wizard. Since task flows show where users will have to perform certain actions, they help clarify the implementation of controls (see later in the chapter). And where decisions have to be made, flows show where menus and information (or affordances) will have to be included.

Use Cases

Programmers have used use cases in the design of software for years. Indeed, it is this tradition that gives use cases some of their power: developers are very accustomed to seeing them and will likely understand them immediately, as will the business people who have over the years had to use them to communicate with programmers. Other design documents, while gaining recognition and acceptance, are simply not as well established.

Use cases are a means of roughing out the functionality of a product or service. A use case attempts to explain in plain language what a certain function does and why.

Uses cases also describe whom the function involves. Cases begin by identifying a set of potential actors. These actors can be based on the personas, but they can even be simpler than that. For example, "the user" can be one of these actors. Another of these actors is typically "the system." The system is the generic actor for any automatic or computing process. It is typically these processes that programmers have been interested in defining, but use cases don't need to be limited to describing events involving the system.

Use cases have the following form:

- ▶ **A title.** This should be descriptive, since it will be referenced often, both in documents and conversation. For example, a use case from an e-mail project might be called "Send an E-mail."

- ▶ **The actors.** Who is performing the function? In the e-mail example, the actors are the user and the system.

- ▶ **The purpose.** What is this use case meant to accomplish and why? For the function sending an e-mail, the purpose would be something like this: "An actor wants to send a message to someone electronically."

- ▶ **The initial condition.** What is happening when the use case starts? In our example, it is simply that the e-mail client is open.

▸ **The terminal condition.** What will happen once the use case ends? In the e-mail example, the condition is again simple: an e-mail has been sent.

▸ **The primary steps.** Discrete moments in this piece of functionality. In the e-mail example, these would be the steps:

1. Actor opens up a new mail window.

2. Actor enters the e-mail address of the recipient or selects it from the address book.

3. Actor enters a subject.

4. Actor enters message.

5. Actor sends mail via some method (for example, a button click).

6. The system checks to make sure the mail has a recipient address.

7. The system closes the mail window.

8. The system sends the mail.

9. The system puts a copy of the mail into the sent mail folder.

▸ **Alternatives.** Alternatives are other use cases that may consider the same or similar functionality. In the e-mail example, Reply to Sender and Forward Mail might be use case alternatives.

▸ **Other use cases used.** Frequently, one piece of functionality is built upon another. List those for reference. The e-mail example includes a few functions that could have their own use cases: Open an E-mail Window, Select an Address from the Address Book, and Confirm Recipient Address might all be separate use cases.

Use cases can be broad (Send an E-mail) or very detailed (Confirm Recipient Address). Use cases can also be very time consuming to create, and a complicated system could potentially have dozens, if not hundreds, of use cases. Use cases are, however, an excellent tool for breaking down tasks and showing what the system will have to support.

Mood Boards

Mood boards (Figure 7.10) are a means for the designer to explore the emotional landscape of a product. Using images, words, colors, typography, and any other means available, the designer crafts a collage that attempts to convey what the final design will feel like. Images and words can be found in magazines and newspapers or online image galleries, or can be created by the designer. Some designers take and use their own photographs for mood boards.

Figure 7.10

Mood boards are one way for designers to consider the emotional content of products.

Traditionally, mood boards were made on large sheets of poster board (thus, the name). The advantage of this approach was that the result could be posted on a wall to be glanced at frequently for inspiration. But this doesn't need to be so. Mood boards can be created digitally: as animations, movies, screen savers, or projections on a wall. The advantage of digital mood boards is that they can include movement and sounds—something traditional paper mood boards obviously cannot do.

The important point is that whatever form the mood board takes, it should reflect *on an emotional level* the feeling the designer is striving for in the product or service. The mood board shouldn't be challenging intellectually; like a good poem or piece of art, it should affect viewers viscerally.

Wireframes

Wireframes (**Figure 7.11**) are a set of documents that show structure, information hierarchy, controls, and content. They have their roots in architectural drawings and network schematics (in fact, they are sometimes called schematics). Next to prototypes, wireframes are usually the most important document that interaction designers produce when working on products. (Services don't typically have wireframes. Instead they have service blueprints; see later in this chapter.) Wireframes are a means of documenting the features of a product, as well as the technical and business logic that went into those features, with only a veneer of visual design (mostly just the functionality's controls). They are the blueprints of a product. Developers, industrial and visual designers, copywriters, and business people use wireframes to understand and build the product in a thoughtful way without being distracted by the visual or physical form.

Wireframes are tricky documents to create because of the multiple audiences that read and use them. Clients want to see how the design meets their business goals. Developers want to see how the product works (and doesn't work—for instance, what happens when an error occurs) so they can know what they need to code. Visual or industrial designers want to see what visual or physical elements will need to be designed, such as the number and type of buttons. Copywriters want to see what they need to write: help text, manuals, headlines, and so on. And designers want to be able to refer to them in the future to remember details such as why there are two buttons instead of one for a certain feature. Accommodating the needs of these various audiences in one document is the designer's task.

In short, the wireframe is an inventory of all the elements that must be accounted for on a particular screen, Web page, or state.

Wireframes typically have three main areas: the wireframe itself, the accompanying annotations, and information about the wireframe (wireframe metadata).

Note: See next page for center controls and states.

Figure 7.11

A wireframe for a desktop music player.

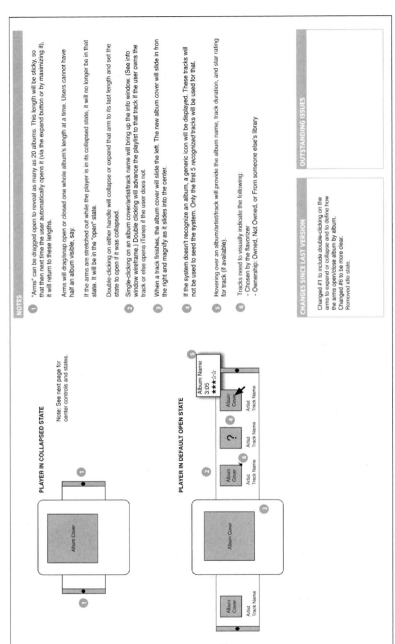

The Wireframe Itself

The wireframe itself is a detailed view of a particular part of a product. Wireframes can show anything from an overview of a product—the form of a PDA, for instance—to detailed documentation of a particular functionality, such as the volume control on a music editing application.

Wireframes should rough out the form of a product. Form is shaped by three factors: the content, the controls necessary to discover and engage with the functionality, and the means of accessing or navigating to those two things. Thus, the wireframe needs to include indicators of content and functions as well as the elements for navigating them (buttons, switches, menus, keystrokes, and so on).

Content is a deliberately vague term that includes text, movies, images, icons, animations, and more. Content strategy is the planning for the creation, publication, and governance of the content that goes into a product.[5] Ideally, any content you are working with will be known before you begin the wireframing process, or at least the specific types and components as determined by the content strategy.

If you don't know the content or have pieces of representative content, you will have to represent it on wireframes by leaving placeholders (usually boxes with an X through them) for images/video and greeked or dummy text. This dummy text is often the one used by typesetters since the 1500s: *Lorem ipsum dolor sit amet, consectetur adipisicing elit, sed do eiusmod tempor incididunt ut labore et dolore magna aliqua.* It's become somewhat of a tradition to use it in wireframes.

Functionality consists of the controls—the buttons, knobs, sliders, dials, input boxes, and so on—of a feature, as well as the accompanying labels and feedback to those controls. A simple Web site form, for example, usually consists of labels ("Enter your name"), text boxes (where you enter your name, for instance), radio buttons ("Male? Female?"), check boxes ("Check here to join our mailing list!"), a Submit button, a Cancel button, and error messages ("You forgot to enter your name!"). All of these need to be documented on the wireframe.

---

5 For more about content strategy, see "The Discipline of Content Strategy" by Kristina Halvorson at www.alistapart.com/articles/thedisciplineofcontentstrategy/ or her book *Content Strategy for the Web*

There also needs to be a way to find and use the content and functionality: navigation. Navigation can consist of any number of methods, such as hyperlinks, simple drop-down menus, toolbars with widgets, and complex manipulations in physical space. On some mobile phones, for instance, pushing the cursor key down while pressing the star key locks the phone. On a digital camera, to view the content (the pictures that were taken), the user may have to change the mode of the camera and then use buttons to flip through the photos.

All these components should appear on the wireframe in a way that shows their general placement and importance. Note that the same wireframe can be used to design many different forms; wireframes can be interpreted in different ways by the visual or industrial designer. What is important is that all the items (content placeholders, functionality, and navigation) needed to create the final product be on the wireframes.

For many products, such as those with small screens or touchscreens, it can make sense to do wireframes drawn to the exact scale of the screen, so that problems do not arise when moving into visual design, prototyping, and production.

Anything on a wireframe that is not obvious or labeled should have a corresponding annotation.

Annotations

Annotations are brief notes that describe nonobvious items on the wireframe. They explain the wireframe when the designer isn't there to do so. When developers or clients want to know the reason for a button, they should be able to read the annotation and understand not just what the button does, but also *why* the button is there. Documenting "why" is a challenge, since annotations should be brief. But there is a vast difference between an annotation that says, "This button stops the process" and one that says, "This button stops the process so users don't have to wait for long periods." In the second version, the reader immediately knows the reason for the button. If a change occurs in the process ("The process now takes only a second"), it's easier to see how to adjust the design appropriately.

Here is a partial list of wireframe objects that should be annotated:

▶   **Controls.** (See later in this chapter for a list of controls.) What happens when a button is pushed or a dial is turned or a hyperlink is clicked.

▶ **Conditional items.** Objects that change based on context. For example, in many application menus, certain items are dimmed depending on what the user is doing at the time.

▶ **Constraints.** Anything with a business, legal, logical, or technical constraint (for example, the longest possible length of a password or the legal reason that minors cannot view certain content).

▶ Anything that, due to space, could not be shown in the wireframe itself (for example, every item on a long drop-down menu).

Wireframe Metadata

Each wireframe should have information about that wireframe—that is, wireframe metadata. Every wireframe should include the following:

▶ **The designer's name.**

▶ **The date the wireframe was made or changed.**

▶ **The version number.**

▶ **What has changed since the last version.** Clients like this; it shows that the designer is actively addressing issues that have arisen during the project.

▶ **Related documentation.** Any related documentation (ideally with a specific page number) that is relevant to this wireframe: business requirements, technical specifications, use cases, and so on. If there are questions about the wireframe ("Did we really say that the robot wouldn't swim?"), appropriate documents can be referenced.

▶ **Unresolved issues.** Are there problems with the wireframe that still need to be decided?

▶ **A place for general notes.** This is the place for the designer to express any final reservations about the product—especially the constraints that affected it. I have occasionally noted where business or technical constraints have had a negative impact on a product and should be addressed. In this way, designers can either argue for changes upon presenting the wireframes, or, if the clients or developers are reluctant to change the constraints, bring them up in the future when complaints arise or another version is planned.

Service Blueprint

Much as wireframes are key documents for digital products, **service blueprints** (**Figure 7.12**) are critical documents for services (which most products are part of anyway). Service blueprints present two major elements: service moments and the service string.

Figure 7.12

A piece of a service blueprint, part of the MAYA Carnegie Library of Pittsburgh project. Service blueprints show not only discrete moments in the service, but also how those moments flow together in a service string.

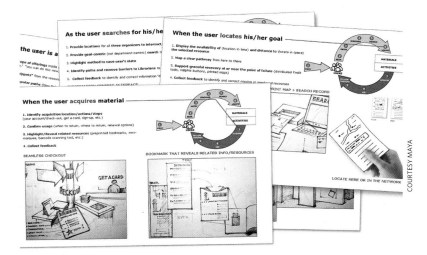

Service Moments

Every service is composed of a set of discrete moments that can be designed. For example, a car wash service has (at least) the following service moments:

- ▶ Customer finds the car wash.

- ▶ Customer enters the car wash.

- ▶ Customer chooses what to have done (washing, waxing, and so on).

- ▶ Customer pays.

- ▶ Car moves into the car wash.

- ▶ Car is washed.

▶ Car is dried.

▶ Interior of the car is cleaned.

▶ Customer leaves the car wash.

Each of these moments can be designed, right down to how the nozzles spray water onto the car. The service blueprint should include all of these moments and present designs for each one. And since there can be multiple paths through a service, there can be multiple designs for each moment. In the car wash scenario, perhaps there are multiple ways of finding the car wash: signs, advertisements, a barker on the street, fliers, and so on.

Here, the list of touchpoints (see chapter 5) can come into play. Which touchpoint is or could be used during each service moment? For each service moment, the touchpoints should be designed. In our car wash example, for instance, the customer paying probably has at least two touchpoints: a sign listing the washing services available and their costs, and some sort of machine or human attendant who takes the customer's money. All of these elements—what the sign says and how it says it, how the machine operates (Does it accept credit cards? How does it make change?), what the attendant says and does—can be designed. A major part of the service blueprints should be the brainstormed ideas for each touchpoint at each service moment. Each service moment should have a concept attached to it, such as the sketches in Figure 7.12 showing a possible check-out kiosk and a bookmark for related library information.

Ideally, each moment should have a sketch or photograph or other rendering of the design, similar to single storyboard frames.

For each service moment, the service blueprint should show what service elements are affected: the environment, objects, process, and people involved. Designers should especially look for service moments that can deliver high value for a low cost. Sometimes small, low-cost changes or additions to a service can quickly provide high value to users. For instance, some airlines found that passengers want a drink as soon as they board. But because other passengers are still boarding and in the aisle, flight attendants cannot offer drink service at that time. The solution was to put a cooler with water bottles at the front of the plane, so that passengers, if they want, can get a drink as they board—a low-cost, high-value solution.

Service String

The second component of a service blueprint is the **service string**. The service string shows the big idea for the service in written and visual form, usually in the form of storyboards. Designers create service strings by putting concepts for various service moments together to form a scenario, or string, of events that provide a pathway through the service.

The service string demonstrates in a vivid way what the pathways through the service will be and provides a comprehensive, big-picture view of the new service. Viewers can see how customers order, pay for, and receive the service, and how employees provide the service. For example, a service string for the earlier car wash example would show in a single scenario customers seeing the new signs, customers using the new machine to pay for the car wash, the special washing service, the attendants who hand-dry the cars, and the new vacuum for cleaning out the cars after they are washed.

Controls

Most applications and devices that interaction designers currently design have some sort of visible controls to manipulate the features of the product—a dial to control volume on a stereo, for example, or a slider to select a date range. (The major exceptions are voice and gestural interactions, discussed later in this chapter.) **Controls** provide both the affordances needed to understand what the product is capable of, and the power to realize that capability.

This section describes many of the basic controls that interaction designers can use as a palette. Almost all of these controls have their own standard feedback mechanisms (a switch moves and stays in its new position, for instance) that interaction designers should consider:

▶ **Switch.** A toggle switch is a very simple control. It moves from one setting ("on") to another ("off") and stays there until changed.

Button. Buttons are the interaction designer's best friend. Once you begin to look for them, it's apparent that buttons are everywhere, all over our interfaces. In a word processing program, there are about 30 buttons visible at any given time. A mobile phone may have about 40 buttons: the number keys for dialing and a keyboard. A button is, at base, a switch that is pressed or clicked to activate it. The button can stay pressed (a **toggle button**), requiring another press to reset it (like most on/off buttons), or it can reset itself automatically (like keys on a keyboard). Buttons can be used for a wide variety of actions: from changing modes (from writing text to drawing, say) to moving an item or a cursor via arrow keys. Buttons can take many forms, from tiny icons to physical squares on a floor that can be stepped on. Buttons, however, are good only for simple actions.

Radio button. Radio buttons enable users to choose from (often preset) items from a set. Typically, these are used to constrain selections, when only one answer is allowed ("What color hair do you have?" Black, Blonde, Red, Brown).

Dial. Dials provide more control than buttons, allowing the user to select a setting along a continuum (such as the amount of heat on a stove's burner) or to choose between different settings or modes (such as the mode for taking pictures and the mode for viewing them on a digital camera. Dials can move freely, or simply turn from an established point to other established points on a wheel. These points are called detents. Some dials, like those often found on clothes driers, can be pushed in and pulled out, performing an action (such as turning on or off) that can vary based on the dial's rotation.

Latch. A latch opens an otherwise tightly closed area. Latches are useful for keeping some areas or items hidden or safe until needed. They are good to use when a button or drop-down menu might be too easy to click or open. For example, latches are frequently used on handheld devices to keep the battery compartment safe.

▶ **Slider.** Sliders, like dials (although linear instead of round), are used for subtle control of a feature, often to control output (such as speaker volume) or the amount of data displayed (such as the number of houses on an interactive map). Sliders with more than one handle can be used to set a range within a range.

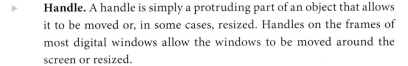

▶ **Handle.** A handle is simply a protruding part of an object that allows it to be moved or, in some cases, resized. Handles on the frames of most digital windows allow the windows to be moved around the screen or resized.

Physical-Only Controls

Some common controls are found only in the physical world and not on screens (although they can certainly manipulate objects on a screen).

▶ **Jog dial.** A jog dial is a type of dial that can be manipulated with a single finger, usually a thumb. It can be dial-like, or it can be a pad of buttons, typically used on small devices for moving a cursor or moving through menus. Jog dials are somewhat difficult to control, especially for young children and the elderly.

▶ **Joystick.** A joystick is a physical device typically used in digital gaming or in other applications that require rapid movement and intensive manipulation of remote physical or digital objects. Joysticks can move in any direction or can be constrained to move only left to right or only up and down.

▶ **Trackball.** A trackball is a physical device for manipulating a cursor or other digital or physical objects. Trackballs are typically in a stationary base, but the ball itself moves in any direction. A computer mouse is often a trackball in a case.

▶ **5-way.** A 5-way is a combination button and cursor. It generally moves a cursor on a screen in four directions (up/down, left/right) and has a button in the center in order to select what has been navigated to.

COURTESY PALM

Bill DeRouchey on Frameworks and Controls

Bill DeRouchey is a Senior Interaction Designer at Ziba Design. Bill has over 15 years of experience as a writer, information architect, product manager, coder, and interaction designer. He has designed a wide variety of products, from handheld satellite radios and medical devices to community Web sites, interactive spaces, and product architectures.

How do you go about choosing a structure or framework for your designs?

Most often, the directions that I explore are largely bounded by the physical constraints at the beginning of the client engagement. Many clients already have specific components selected for manufacturing before engaging with them, so I have to treat those as givens, specific display dimensions and resolutions being the most common example. When you're given a 160x128 pixel space to work within, that tends to inform your structure quite a bit.

Beyond that, my designs tend to follow a pattern of reminiscence. A new medical monitor needs to behave like clinicians are used to them behaving. New satellite radios need to convey reminiscent qualities of "radio" so that people have a basis from which they approach the device. It's all about giving people a head start for understanding how to interact with the new product in front of them. This allows it to better fit into their lives as seamlessly as possible.

You've written a lot about the history of the button. Why is that important?

Interaction design existed as an activity decades before it was explicitly named as one. Industrial designers applied knobs, switches, and buttons to their products, and determined how they would be used by consumers. So these products created a rich history of people interacting with technology long before computers entered our daily lives. These first decades of products paved the way and formed our expectations of interacting with products.

This is where the button gets interesting. Consider that our main concern as interaction designers today is how we interact with products. In the early days, the question was why we should interact with products at all? Convenience, luxury, efficiency and visions of the leisurely future were all used as aspirational triggers to buy blenders, washers, radios, and more. And all of this aspiration was communicated via imagery of fingers pushing buttons.

Bill DeRouchey on Frameworks and Controls *(continued)*

The phrase "push-button" itself meant easy, simple, even-you-can-use-this product. That's a lot of social burden placed on a single UI widget, which is why I love this story.

What should interaction designers know about controls?

Physical controls have strong metaphors and history attached to them. Knobs and sliders typically indicate that you're looking for something vague along a spectrum: the right volume or temperature setting. Buttons and switches typically indicate a choice is being made. Turn the lights on. Start the microwave. Controls usually do only one thing.

Accordingly, one of the biggest challenges of controls is that space, size, and cost limit you for how many features are important enough to warrant their own physical controls. Do you really need to adjust bass levels that often, or do you bury that feature in another control somehow? Like all design, it's a delicate dance to determine this hierarchy, and the best way to solve it is to put prototypes in front of other people.

What are the most important things to remember when laying out controls?

Laying controls requires a strong sense of hierarchy, zoning, and priority. Control panels typically focus on a tight set of tasks, with one hero task in that set. In air conditioners, changing temperature is more important than adjusting schedules. In radios, adjusting volume is the hero task. These controls should be larger, offset, or otherwise designed to have the highest priority. It should be clear to people what is the single most important thing to do. Determine your hero task.

A common mistake is designing all the controls with an overly uniform look and feel. It may look clean to have 12 different buttons with uniform shape and color lined up into a grid, but that approach offers no quick visual appraisal to determine what control does what. In these situations, the labels become more important, creating a secondary problem.

Digital-Only Controls

While many controls are found in both the physical, analog world and the digital one, some controls are only found on screens. These digital controls have grown from the original graphical user interface (GUI) vocabulary that was invented at Xerox PARC in the 1970s, reinvented in the 1980s in the Macintosh and PC operating systems, and added to and expanded by Web conventions in the 1990s:

▸   **Check box**. A check box enables users to select items from a short list.

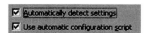

▸   **Twist.** Twists turn up or down, either revealing or hiding content or a menu in a panel.

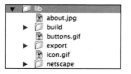

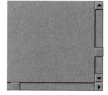

▸   **Scroll bar.** Scroll bars enable users to move content within a particular window or panel. Scroll bars can be vertical or horizontal. Scroll bars themselves can be manipulated via the cursor or buttons (for instance, by using arrow keys).

▸   **Drop-down menu.** Drop-down menus allow designers to cluster navigation, functionality, or content together without having to display it all at once. Drop-down menus can be displayed by rolling over them, or they can be opened with a click. They can retract after a selection has been made or the cursor rolls off them, though not necessarily.

- ▶ **Multiple-selection list (or list box).** Multiple-selection lists enable users to select multiple items in a list.

- ▶ **Text box**. Text boxes enable users to enter numbers, letters, or symbols. They can be as small as (and constrained to) a single character or as large as the whole screen.

- ▶ **Spin box.** Spin boxes are text boxes with additional controls that enable users to manipulate what is inside the text box without having to type a value. They are good for suggesting values in what otherwise might be an ambiguous text box.

The combination of one (and usually more) controls plus the system response is called a **widget**. Widgets are the building blocks of any application or device. An MP3 player, for instance, is made of widgets: one for controlling volume, one for controlling the playing of music files, one for organizing files, one for exporting files, and so on. In each case, the user uses controls to perform an action, and the system responds. All applications and devices are made up of widgets.

Non-traditional Inputs

We are arriving at a time when keyboards, mice, and styluses aren't the only—and possibly not even the primary—way we interact with the digital world. With the dawn of ubiquitous computing, interactive environments, and sensor-enabled devices (see Chapter 9), people will engage with many different sorts of objects that have microprocessors and sensors built into them, from rooms to appliances to bicycles.

The controls for these faceless interfaces are the human body: our voices, our movements, and simply our presence.

Figure 7.13

The author screams at Kelly Dobson's Blendie, a voice-controlled blender, to get it to frappé.

Voice

Widespread implementation of **voice**-controlled systems has been on the horizon for at least a decade now. For now, voice-controlled interfaces are most prevalent (naturally) on phone systems and mobile phones. For example, people call their banks and perform transactions or dial their mobile phones with just their voices. Voice commands typically control limited functionality, and the device typically has to be ready to receive voice commands, either because it only functions via voice commands (as with automated phone systems and some voice-controlled devices—see **Figure 7.13**), or because it has been prepared to receive voice commands, as with mobile phones that allow voice-dialing.

Gestures

To most computers and devices, people consist of two things: hands and eyes. The rest of the human body is ignored. But as our devices gain more awareness of the movement of the human body through sensors such as cameras, the better able they will be to respond to the complete human body, including **gestures**. Devices like the Wii and the iPhone with their built-in accelerometers allow for all manner of new ways of controlling our devices via movements in space. See **Figure 7.14**.

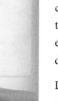

Figure 7.14

This gestural entertainment center uses a camera from Canesta to detect gestures in space that control the television.

Designers need to be especially aware of several issues when designing gestural interfaces:

▶ **Physiology and kinesiology.** Designers have to know how humans move and what the limitations are for that movement. For example, holding an arm out and making gestures can be quickly tiring—a condition known as "gorilla arm."

▶ **Presence and instruction.** Since there might be no visible interface—for example, consider the hands-free paper towel dispenser in many public restrooms—letting users know a gestural device is there and how to use it needs to be addressed.

▶ **Avoiding "false positives."** Since human beings make gestures all the time in the course of just moving around, designing and then detecting deliberate gestures can be challenging.

► **Matching gesture to task.** Without standard controls, figuring out the best motion to trigger an action is important. Simple gestures should be matched to simple tasks.

Presence

Some systems respond simply to a person's **presence**. Many interactive games and installations such as Daniel Rozin's "Wooden Mirror" (**Figure 7.15**) respond to a body's being near their sensors.

Figure 7.15

The "Wooden Mirror" creates the image of what is in front of it (seen by a camera) by flipping wooden blocks within its frame.

There are many design decisions to be made with presence-activated systems. Consider a room with sensors and environmental controls, for example. Does the system respond immediately when someone enters the room, turning on lights and climate-control systems, or does it pause for a few moments, in case someone was just passing through?

In addition, sometimes users may not want to be known to be present. Users may not want their activities and location known for any number of reasons, including personal safety and simple privacy. Designers will have to determine how and when a user can become "invisible" to presence-activated systems.

Summary

Refinement of design concepts is about making smart, deliberate choices about how the concept would work and could be built given the known constraints. It's about using the known laws of interaction design to guide design choices, and about putting in the right affordances and feedback so that users can create the right mental model of the product in order to properly use it.

Of course, right now, these are just documents; they don't live and breathe and you cannot really "interact" with them. For that, prototyping is necessary, and that is what the next chapter covers.

For Further Reading

About Face 3: The Essentials of Interaction Design, Alan Cooper, Robert Reimann, and David Cronin

The Design of Everyday Things, Donald A. Norman

Designing for the Digital Age: How to Create Human-Centered Products and Services, Kim Goodwin

Designing Interfaces: Patterns for Effective Interaction Design, Jenifer Tidwell

Designing Gestural Interfaces, Dan Saffer

Designing Web Interfaces: Principles and Patterns for Rich Interactions, Bill Scott and Theresa Neil

Mobile Interaction Design, Matt Jones and Gary Marsden

Communicating Design: Developing Web Site Documentation for Design and Planning, Dan Brown

Designing the Obvious: A Common Sense Approach to Web Application Design, Robert Hoekman Jr.

Information Architecture for the World Wide Web: Designing Large-Scale Web Sites, Louis Rosenfeld and Peter Morville

Ambient Findability: What We Find Changes Who We Become, Peter Morville

Content Strategy for the Web, Kristina Halvorson

8

Prototyping, Testing, and Development

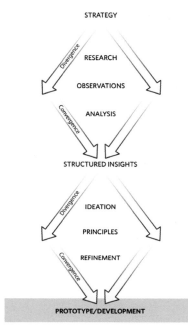

Once you have worked out some or many of the details (or even before), it is time to prototype and actually build the product. This phase of design is about refining the parts of the design that cannot be easily done with paper documentation, namely timing, animation, movement, and interaction.

One of the first things you must consider when prototyping is the interface design.

Interface Design

We can engage with digital products only through some sort of interface. Although there have been some strides in the field of Brain-Computer Interface, most of us cannot yet connect to digital devices through a cable directly from our brains to microprocessors. For now, we need some intermediary to communicate between us and our digital devices: an interface.

Interface design is so closely tied to interaction design that many believe they are the same thing, which isn't exactly true. Interface design is the *experienced representation* of the interaction design, not the interaction design itself. The interface is what people see, hear, or feel, and while it is immensely important, it is only a part of interaction design.

Digital products are a bit like icebergs. The part that can be seen (the interface) is really just the tip; what's below the surface, what isn't seen, is where the main part of the interaction design lies: the design decisions that the designer has made and the technical underpinnings that make the interface a reality. An interface is where the interaction designer's choices about how people can engage with a product and how that product or service should respond are realized. In other words, the interface is where the invisible functionality of a product is made visible (often via affordances—see Chapter 7 for more information), accessible, and usable.

In the past, form often closely followed function. A hammer looks the way it does because its shape is optimal for driving in nails. With digital devices, however, form doesn't necessarily follow function. Objects on a screen can have any shape and can potentially serve any purpose. For example, an unlabeled button sitting in the middle of a Web page could look like an elephant, a tea cup, or even like, well, a button, and clicking it could open another Web page, start an animation, play music, close the browser window, or do a variety of other things. Likewise, the physical form of an object may have nothing to do with the behavior it can exhibit. A round orb can do anything from control your TV to alert you that a stock is falling. When working with digital devices, the interaction designer has a lot more fluidity and ambiguity to account for.

What interaction designers are most concerned about with interface design is generally the layout and placement of controls and navigation. For hardware/software products, a functional cartography (see Chapter 7) should be performed to figure out what controls go where.

Onscreen, designers need to provide cues regarding where the user should look. Color can be used to attract the eye, as can contrasting fonts (larger, bold, and so on). Lines and boxes can group objects together, but these should be used sparingly, lest the users focus on the lines and boxes and not the features—try to use whitespace instead.

In the Western world, the eye generally travels from left to right, top to bottom, and designers should be aware of this flow and design for it. Don't force users' eyes to jump all over the screen.

When objects are close together, Gestalt psychology tells us, the mind will assume that they are related. This is a good thing when designers want objects to seem related—for example, a Submit button next to a text box—but not so good when the pieces of functionality drifting into each other are unrelated.

Positioning and alignment of objects are also important. Objects that are aligned will appear to be related, and objects should ideally be aligned horizontally and vertically to create a clean look. Objects that are indented beneath other objects will appear to be subordinate to those above them, and objects near the top of the screen will generally seem more important than those farther down.

Designers should always perform the squint test on their visual interfaces. By squinting at the screen, designers can optically smudge the details and see which items on the screen have prominence. This test can often lead to surprise, revealing that secondary or unimportant items seem overly important in the design. The squint test helps ensure that the layout is strong.

Luke Wroblewski on Interface Design

Luke Wroblewski is an interface designer, strategist, and author of the books Site-Seeing: A Visual Approach to Web Usability *and* Web Form Design. *He is currently Senior Director of Product Ideation & Design at Yahoo!.*

How can visual design support (or detract) from interaction design?

In most applications, audio cues need to be used sparingly and instructional text is rarely read. As a result, the visual design bears the responsibility of communicating the possibilities, limitations, and state of interactions. It tells users what they are seeing, how it works, and why they should care.

When visual elements are applied without an understanding of the underlying interactions they are meant to support, however, the wrong message may be sent to users. Visual styling that obscures or clouds crucial interaction options, barriers, or status messages can have a significantly negative impact on user experience.

Think of visual design as the "voice" of interaction design and information architecture. It communicates the importance of (and relationships between) the content and actions within an application.

What do interaction designers need to know about visual design?

Visual design can be thought of as two interwoven parts: visual organization and personality. Visual organization utilizes the principles of perception (how we make sense of what we see) to construct a visual narrative. Through applications of contrast, visual designers can communicate the steps required to complete a task, the relationships between information, or the hierarchy between interface elements. So clearly visual organization is a key component for successful interface designs.

Unfortunately, most discussions about the effectiveness of visual design don't focus on visual organization systems. Instead, they are limited to a subjective analysis of the personality (look and feel) of an interface. Personality is achieved through a judicious selection of colors, fonts, patterns, images, and visual elements designed to communicate a particular message to an audience. But just about everyone has a color or font preference, so when asked to evaluate visual design that's where they turn first.

My advice to interaction designers is to take the time to learn the principles underlying visual organization. You'll be better able to communicate with the visual designers on your team and, more importantly, with the end users of your product.

What are some of the common interface mistakes that new interaction designers make?

The most common interface design mistakes I see are overstatements of visual contrast. For example, designers will want to make sure everything on a screen can be found and therefore apply an equal amount of visual weight to each element to ensure it's "discoverable." The problem is when every element on a screen is shouting to get noticed, no one gets heard. As a user, you can recognize these types of designs because your eyes bounce from one element to the next. There is no hierarchy and as a result no flow through the content and actions on the screen.

Similarly, many designers will overemphasize the differences between individual interface elements through multiple visual relationships: different font, size, color, and alignment. You don't need excess visual contrast to distinguish objects or make things findable. Think about ways to "eliminate the unnecessary so that the necessary may speak" and aim for the least effective difference between elements.

You talk a lot about personality. How do you provide a visual personality to your designs?

Whether you've thought about it or not, people will ascribe a personality to your product based on the way it looks and acts. Therefore, it is in your best interest to be aware of the personality you are creating for your site through visual design (or lack of it) and make certain it is telling the story you want.

Luckily, there's a huge visual vocabulary available for establishing an appropriate personality for your application. Millions of colors, hundreds of thousands of font choices, and innumerable patterns and images are all at your disposal. The trick is settling on the right combination of these for your particular needs. Consider what you want to communicate to your audience and how; then locate visual elements that convey that message in the world around you. You'll be surprised at what you can find when you look!

Sound Effects

Sound is both over- and under-used in interaction design. Nearly everyone has had the experience of going to a Web site only to have it suddenly blast music, sending you scrambling to turn the thing off. But sound effects, done well, can subtly enhance an interface.

Sounds can be ambient cues that something has happened so that users don't have to constantly monitor the application for changes. This use of sound is especially helpful in applications with frequent changes that may occur while the user is otherwise occupied. A ding indicates that an e-mail has arrived. The door-opening sound indicates that a buddy has signed onto the instant messenger client. The ring of a mobile phone indicates that a text message has arrived. These are all helpful sound cues.

How can you tell if a sound will, over time, become an annoyance? Record it. Test it on others and see what they think. Listen to it frequently. Use the application yourself and see if you become annoyed at it. If you do, probably others will as well.

Prototyping

Aside from the finished product, prototypes are the ultimate expression of the interaction designer's vision. The importance of prototypes cannot be over-estimated. Indeed, many designers feel that prototyping is *the* design activity, that everything before it is but a prelude, and that to design *is* to prototype.

Prototyping is where, finally, all the pieces of the design come together in a holistic unit. Indeed, many people will have difficulty understanding a design until they see and use the prototype. Like all the other models and diagrams, they are a tool for communicating. Prototypes communicate the message "This is what it could be like."

What form these prototypes take depends on both the designer's resources and the type of product or service that is being designed. A designer with the right resources can produce some high-fidelity prototypes that look and behave just like the final product or service would. Many retail chains build whole prototype stores, for example.

Todd Zaki Warfel on Prototyping

Todd Zaki Warfel is a founding partner at Messagefirst, where he focuses on design and research for consumer and Business-to-Business products. With over 16 years of industry experience, Todd has been fortunate enough to create over 15 industry-first products. He is the author of the book A Practitioner's Guide to Prototyping.

Why should interaction designers prototype anything? Why not just jump from concept to development?

Prototyping is a great way to work through your design concepts. With wireframes and Photoshop comps, the interactions are missing. This is especially problematic with dynamic transitions. Instead of being able to show the actual interaction, you're left to describe. In lieu of a prototype, I've often found myself whiteboarding and waving my hands in the air to describe a particular transition. I find it easier just to pick up some paper, draw on it, fold and tear it, and make a mini prototype to show the intended interaction.

When jumping directly from concept to development, you risk leaving the interpretation of your intended interaction up to engineers. They are more likely to take the route of least resistance (a.k.a easiest to code), which is most likely not the originally intended interaction.

The biggest benefit—besides working through your design—to prototyping? You create a clearer vision among the team. You get to show and tell and not rely on imagination and misinterpretation.

What should interaction designers prototype?

You don't have to prototype everything—it's a prototype. And prototypes, by definition, are incomplete.

It's important not to fall into the trap of trying to prototype the entire system. I typically pick out 5 or 6 key scenarios I want to focus on at a single time. I'll prototype only what I need to communicate the most important aspects of that concept, things that might not be explicit in the design, or transitions that have some type of wow factor, or impact the user experience.

Todd Zaki Warfel on Prototyping *(continued)*

If I have 2 or 3 really solid concepts I want to explore, then I might prototype the 2 or 3 different solutions and do A/B testing to see which one performs best. Sometimes, I intentionally leave holes in the prototype, to elicit design ideas from participants. When they come across an aspect that isn't fleshed out, I'll ask them "How would you expect that to work?"

What are some of the difficulties with prototyping?

Deciding what pieces to prototype and how deep to go. It's that balancing act of getting the right amount, without doing too much.

The most common mistake is not setting expectations appropriately. If you don't set expectations of the stakeholders you're demoing your prototyping to, then you're going to end up spending 20 minutes defending the parts you left out. If you tell them upfront that this version is going to focus on the drag-and-drop features of the shopping cart, but that address verification isn't included in this round, then your audience will focus on the shopping cart interactions and not get hung up on field verification issues. It's really a bit of selling it appropriately.

What level of fidelity should interaction designers prototype at?

The right level. I know it's a bit of a cop-out answer, but that all really depends on the audience and intent of your prototype. If you're prototyping to show another designer, then something rough and low fidelity might be best. If you're going to demo it to the CEO, then you probably need something a bit more polished.

Be careful about going too polished early on, as you risk customers not giving feedback. Prototypes that are too complete can leave the CEO thinking that all you have to do is ship it, or customers thinking all the design decisions have been made.

How can designers get the most out of prototyping?

Take a page from Nike's book and just do it. I was nervous the first time I started prototyping—frankly, I was probably in way over my head. But I figured it out. The more I prototyped, the easier it got. And now, even when faced with some seemingly impossible designs to execute, I know I'll find a way to figure it out.

The best way to get the most out of prototyping is to just starting doing it. Once you start, you'll never turn back, and you'll wonder how you ever got by without it.

Ideally, designers will create multiple prototypes, or at least multiple variations that can be played with and tested. Designers use prototypes to experiment and see what works—for the designer, for clients, and for users. Frequently, one prototype is clearly the right approach, but just as often, after testing, it becomes clear that parts of each prototype work well, and the designer has to shape these into another prototype that is a hybrid of the best of the earlier prototypes.

Prototypes fall somewhere on a continuum of low- to high-fidelity. The type of prototype you build should depend upon the type of feedback you want to receive. If you want to evaluate overall functionality and product flow, low-fidelity prototypes are appropriate. For more detail on elements such as look and feel and animation, high-fidelity prototypes are more appropriate.

Low-Fidelity Prototypes

Low-fidelity prototypes are put together quickly and are usually crude and unpolished. They might be sketched on paper, made out of cardboard, or perhaps digital but with limited functionality and a basic interface. Low-fidelity prototypes frequently don't "work"—that is, they're usually static with no real interactivity at all. They require people to make them function, by faking any system behavior. Low-fidelity prototypes are meant to be put together (and thrown away) quickly: in just enough time to test a concept.

Since low-fidelity prototypes are not or only somewhat interactive, they usually require someone to be controlling them in order to make them appear interactive. This is called **Wizard of Oz manipulation**, because "the man behind the curtain" (usually the designer) has to make the product seem interactive, either by flipping pages of the paper prototype or by controlling how the digital screen reacts (by flipping to a particular screen when a user pushes a button, for example).

Paper Prototypes

The simplest forms of prototypes are those on paper. Because they aren't digital, some have argued they aren't prototypes at all, but paper prototypes (**Figure 8.1**) do have value for testing the product's overall concept and flow. Indeed, the very fact they aren't digital means that "users" have no expectations that this is the finished product and so are free to comment on them critically.

Figure 8.1

This to-scale, paper prototype of a touchscreen phone was tested with users alongside the physical form.

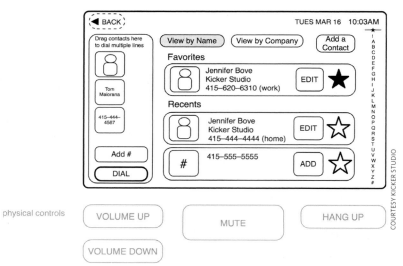

Paper prototypes are usually the fastest way to demonstrate a working product. On paper, the designer creates a walkthrough of the product or system. Each piece of paper contains one moment of the design. That moment can be a Web page, a screen, or a state. Users, aided by the designers, can step through the prototype by flipping through the pages in a particular order. Pages should be numbered, and instructions for moving between the pages should be provided ("If you 'press' this button, go to page 9").

During testing (described in the next section), the subjects or the designer can write comments and notes directly on the prototype ("I really want this button to be *here*"). Even though they are rough, paper prototypes should be done to scale when possible. It is easy to create impractical interfaces otherwise.

Physical Prototypes

Physical prototypes (**Figure 8.2**) can be made for simple parts of a design (such as a dial or a button) or they can be representations of the whole device. Appliances, consumer electronics, control panels, and mobile and medical devices need to have their physical form prototyped alongside the screen whenever possible (using the functional cartography detailed in Chapter 7) simply because there is more to the experience of using a device than just the screen itself. A device's physical form—especially when it is held in the hand—can drastically change both its behavior and the behaviors of its users.

Figure 8.2

These physical prototypes of a small mobile device did variations on size, grip, stylus, and overall shape.

Low-fidelity physical prototypes can be made of almost anything: wood, paper, cardboard, clay, plastic, foamcore…just to name a few materials. For low-fidelity prototypes what is important is the suggestion of form and the location and kind of controls and sensors, as well as size, shape, and weight.

High-Fidelity Prototypes

Once the general concepts, product forms, and task flows have been prototyped using low-fidelity methods, it is time to focus on making a **high-fidelity prototype** (**Figure 8.3**). As the name suggests, these prototypes require a more serious investment in time and resources to create.

Figure 8.3

Purely digital prototypes like this one can be easily distributed on the Web.

Unlike a low-fidelity prototype, the high-fidelity prototype mostly works as it should. When a user turns a dial, something happens that doesn't require Wizard of Oz trickery to make it work. The data might not be live, but product mostly behaves as it would in the field, and contains as many of the product details as possible: in interaction, environmental, industrial, and visual design, as well as in engineering and code.

Aesthetics matter when crafting high-fidelity prototypes. Even though it only occurs occasionally, the prototype should be nearly indistinguishable from the product a user would buy or encounter. The less the high-fidelity prototype seems like a prototype, the more accurate the feedback will be. Users shouldn't be confused at being handed a stack of papers and a cardboard box and told to imagine it is an in-store retail kiosk.

For complex functionality, the richer and more complete a designer can make the high-fidelity prototype, the better. It is hard for users to imagine how, for example, a tool to draw boxes might work without actually being able to play with it and draw boxes themselves.

The danger with a high-fidelity prototype is that both users and clients may think it is the final product. Expectations should be properly set for what the prototype actually is: a prototype.

Service Prototypes

Prototyping a service usually isn't much like prototyping a product. Since both the process and people are so important to services, services don't really come alive until people are using the service and walking through the process. Prototyping a service typically involves creating scenarios based on the service moments outlined in the service blueprint and acting them out with clients and stakeholders, playing out the scenarios as theatre. Seriously.

Role playing constitutes a significant part of the service design process. Only through enactments can designers really determine how the service will feel. Someone (often the designer) is cast in the role of employee, while others play the roles of customers. This prototyping can make use of a script or an outline of a script, or the enactments can simply be improvised. The players act their way through a service string to demonstrate how the service works.

Ideally, these scenarios will be played within a mock-up of the environment (**Figure 8.4**), with prototypes of the objects involved as well. Only in this

Figure 8.4

A prototype of a subway service, created by projecting images behind the designers/actors.

way can the flow and feeling of the service really be known. Environments can be simulated using giant foam blocks for objects, masking tape on the floor to block out areas, images projected on walls, and so on.

One alternative ("Wikitecture") some designers and architects are experimenting with for prototyping spaces is to model environments in a virtual world such as Second Life.[1]

Services also can be prototyped using a live environment with real customers and employees. The Mayo Clinic's SPARC program does this (see the case study that follows), as do many retail stores, using pilot programs at a small number of locations. These prototypes are, of course, extremely high fidelity, working exactly as the actual service would because they involve actual customers. Although it is certainly best to start with low-fidelity service prototypes (if only because of the cost), eventually the service will need to be tested with actual customers and employees, either in a prototype/pilot environment or live, making adjustments as the service lives.

Testing

Once you have a prototype, the product or service should be tested with users. This process is usually called user testing, but that's really a misnomer; it's the product or service that's being tested, not the users (**Figure 8.5**).

The same rules that guide design research (see Chapter 4) also guide testing: you go to the users, you talk to them, you write things down. Unless what is being tested is a service that requires a prototyped space or some other significant setup, testing is best done in the subject's own environment: on the subject's computer, in the subject's home or office, in the subject's city or town.

Figure 8.5

A digital prototype being tested by a user at home.

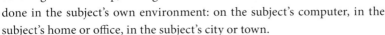

1   See The Arch, a blog by Jon Brouchoud at http://archsl.wordpress.com/

Case Study: Electronic Check-In System

The Company

The Mayo Clinic, an internationally-known medical facility.

The Problem

Even though the delivery of health care hasn't changed much in 50 years, most patient satisfaction about health care comes through the delivery of that care, not necessarily the care's effectiveness. Designers at the Mayo Clinic observed that a point of patient annoyance is checking-in simply to say that they had arrived. The check-in process sometimes even exacerbates medical conditions.

The Process

The Mayo Clinic's SPARC (See, Plan, Act, Refine, Communicate) program was created for just such a situation as the check-in process. SPARC provides live-environment (real patients, real doctors) exploration and experimentation to support the design and development of

innovations in health-care delivery. SPARC is both a physical space and a methodology combining design and scientific rigor. Embedded within a clinical practice in the hospital, the SPARC space has modular furniture and movable walls that allow many different configurations, and it is staffed with a blend of physicians, business professionals, and designers. Using the airline industry as a model, SPARC designed a prototype of a check-in kiosk, collected initial feedback from potential users, and then iteratively refined that prototype.

The Solution

SPARC designed a self-check-in service similar to airline check-in services at airports. Patients check in using a kiosk instead of waiting in a line just to say that they have arrived. SPARC tested the kiosk with 100 patients and found a high rate of acceptance and significant reduction in the number of interactions required while the patient is waiting for service. There was also a marked reduction in patients' waiting time.

Testing labs do have two advantages: efficiency and a controlled environment. The designer can quickly see many subjects in a single day, one after the other, without having to change location, and there is only one setup.

Also similarly to design research, subjects need to be recruited, and a moderator script (also known in this stage as a **test plan** or **testing protocol**) devised. In the test plan, a "route" through the product that tests the functionality and feedback is devised, as well as questions that would prompt (although not guide) users through the system. Strive for neutral questions such as, "If you wanted to check your account balance, what would you do?"

Test plans also have to take into account the limitations of the prototype. Often, prototypes do not use live data, so only certain kinds of input will work properly, and often only certain pathways through the system have been built. For example, to get to a particular page, users will have to search for a particular name. Other names won't work, so the moderator may have to prompt the subject to enter that particular name.

A/B testing (sometimes called "bucket testing") is a particular method of testing wherein two different designs are shown to users, and then the results compared to see if one is markedly better than the other.

Testing is also the time when any wrong conclusions reached during design research can be corrected. Designers may find that they misinterpreted the research or drew the wrong implications from the research. By talking to users during testing, they can clear up those misconceptions. Ideally, designers will carry a set of wireframes and other documents during testing and make notes right there about any patterns they see. For example, if users keep stumbling while attempting to complete a registration form, the designer should plan to revise that form later.

Designers, when testing, should not be defensive about their designs; indeed, it is often best for the designer to allow other team members or usability specialists to conduct the testing while they simply observe and take notes. The human tendency is to nudge subjects ("Why don't you just look over there at that button?") because the designer knows the design better than the subject. To avoid inhibiting testers, designers should avoid identifying themselves as the product's designer. Knowing that the designer is present may cause testers to change or soften their feedback.

Test results can be delivered in an **opportunity report**, which indicates where in the product users had trouble, and also possible suggestions for improvement based on test results and/or subject suggestions.

Most experienced designers know one truism: you seldom get it right the first time. Testing will reveal the flaws, both known and unknown. Nothing is more humbling for designers than watching users stumble through their designs. While testing, good designers watch for the same thing they watched for in design research: patterns. Then they go back to the wireframes and prototypes and fix the errors. Then they test them again. This is how products and services should be made.

Heuristic Evaluation

If you don't have the resources to do testing with users, the least you can do is perform a heuristic evaluation on the prototype yourself. Walk through the prototype as though you hadn't designed it and didn't already know everything about it and why features are the way they are. Look for the following things:

- **There are too many actions, clicks, or steps to do key features.** This indicates that important functionality is buried or inefficient. Consider redoing the framework or task flows.

- **Lack of explanation.** If you wonder why you are performing a task, it's guaranteed users will wonder, too. Either information (a label, a description, a process indicator such as "You are on Step 3 of 4") needs to be provided, or the feature needs to be rethought from a strategy or framework perspective—for example, do you really need this feature?

- **Huh? What just happened?** If you don't understand the result of an action, the feedback and/or feedforward are likely poor.

- **Did anything just happen?** If you or the system performs an action and you can't tell, the feedback is inadequate.

- **Hidden features.** Are there features that are difficult or impossible to find? Are there functions hidden in modes that should be surfaced to the top? Review information architecture/frameworks.

▶ **Lost.** If you are somewhere in the system and can't figure out where you are or how to get back, it's an information architecture/navigation problem.

▶ **Where's my data?** We expect a system to remember basic things about us, and especially things that we have taken the time to tell it (user information, settings, and so on). When data isn't there, it can cause anger, frustration, and concern.

▶ **If I click this, what happens?** If you can't tell what is going to happen when you press a submit button or flip a switch, the feedforward/label is bad. This can also speak to a lack of understanding of a feature's purpose.

▶ **I didn't see that button.** If a key control isn't visible, the layout, visual hierarchy, or affordances are poor.

▶ **Dead ends.** Error messages, becoming trapped in a feature or mode, or being unable to undo an action are signs that the task flow could be bad.

All of these situations can trip users up and should be avoided.

Development

The final step before the product or project is launched is the actual development—and, for physical objects, manufacturing. Once in this stage, the designer's role (unless he is also the developer) is one of troubleshooting, tweaking the design to fit the code and/or the physical materials, and collaboration.

Essentially, the designer should be part of the development process in order to ensure that the product comes out as envisioned. Once the building process has begun, assuredly issues will arise that had not been thought of, and designers should make themselves available to work through those issues alongside the developers.

Leisa Reichelt on Designing Throughout the Development Process

Leisa Reichelt is a contextual researcher and user-centered designer who has been designing for over a decade, with her most recent and public project being Drupal 7. She also coined the term "ambient intimacy" to describe that sense of connectedness that you get from participating in social tools online that allow you to feel as though you are maintaining and, perhaps, in fact, increasing your closeness with people in your social network.

Why should designers bother with being involved in the development process?

Firstly, the design process is the development process and the development process is the design process. The idea that they are separate from each other is a tragic misconception.

Design decisions happen well beyond the end of what we'd traditionally recognize as the "design phase" of a project—if you want to be a part of this ongoing design decision-making then you need to be there when the decisions are being made.

This happens when developers interpret your specifications, when they assume you must have meant something different because what you've done looks nuts to them, when they find something that hasn't been specified at all and make it work how they think it should work. It's not a failing in your specification that these things happen, it's just the way it works. You can acknowledge this and get involved or you can forever wonder why things never leave the developers looking and working like you want them to...your call.

Secondly, it's about knowing your media. You'd be horrified if you asked an architect to design you a house and she knew nothing about the materials she was specifying. Similarly, you should know about the materials that you're using in your design—this includes the code. You don't need to know exactly how to code up your designs but by working closely with developers you learn about the capabilities, potential, and restrictions of your media. This can only help you be a better designer.

There is a lot of talk about how design fits into the Agile development process. How do you see that?

Unfortunately it is often a whole world of pain. Agile is a really great idea in many ways but it was born of developers and, unfortunately, the vast majority of Agile projects are still very much

Leisa Reichelt on Designing Throughout the Development Process *(continued)*

development-led. This means that there is very little room for designers to work in an Agile way and many developers are actually really uncomfortable working with designers who are also working Agile and therefore don't know the whole story of what we're building yet either!

There is a lot of great work being done, and a lot still to happen, to try to get design to work better in an Agile environment, but it is still very much a work in progress. What we do know is that it is all but impossible to do good design work whilst trying to fit into a traditional strict Agile method—we as designers need to engage more in trying to shape the methodologies so that they better suit our work practices, and then talk to each other about what works and what doesn't so we can start to develop a better shared understanding and get a design-friendly version of Agile out there!

What's the "washing machine" development process you advocate?

It's a kind of silly term with a sketchy diagram that I use to describe the way that we need to mess with Agile so that design fits into it better.

There are many great things about Agile that should support good design—the emphasis on prototyping (creating working releases), incremental work, working to user stories, working collaboratively, short bursts of high focus—all of these should contribute to good design outcomes. There are other aspects of good design practice that need to be integrated better into Agile though. For example, involving real end users rather than just end user representatives, allowing designers a period of time (that we're now calling Iteration Zero) to conduct research, to come up with an overall design framework, and to allow for more iterative work—you don't see enough iteration in most Agile projects.

What's the best way of seeing your design make its way through the development process and end up working like you'd imagined it?

I think perhaps to spend less time imagining it and more time being there, making it happen. What I'm really aiming to do these days is as little upfront documentation as possible, but rather to work closely with the developers as early as possible to start getting things built—and with the time that I would have otherwise spent annotating wireframes, I get to work with the developers to fine tune the design and interaction, to do more iteration. I'm not sure if it's just that I do less imagining at the beginning so I get less disappointed at the end! I don't think so. I think it's just a much more satisfactory way to work.

Case Study: Revelation PROJECT

The Company

Revelation, a Web application startup that provides software and services for qualitative researchers.

The Problem

Revelation's product PROJECT, a Web application for researchers to set up daily diaries, photo essays, questionnaires, and other creative stimuli for their study participants, in its first iteration had some significant usability and performance problems that were causing issues for their users. Revelation wanted a new version of PROJECT before a major industry event, so rapid results were required.

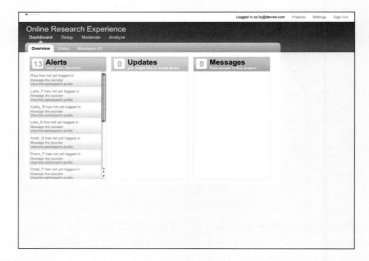

The Process

Working with design firm Devise, Revelation did ethnographic research in two locations with 10 researchers who conducted a mix of market research and design research. The team ultimately created six personas from their research: a market researcher, a design researcher, a client observer (the person requesting and paying the researcher to do the work who gets to do certain things in the system), two study participants, and the recruiter (the person who would find and put participants into PROJECT on behalf of the researcher). The personas, placed into scenarios, drove the new design.

Case Study: Revelation PROJECT *(continued)*

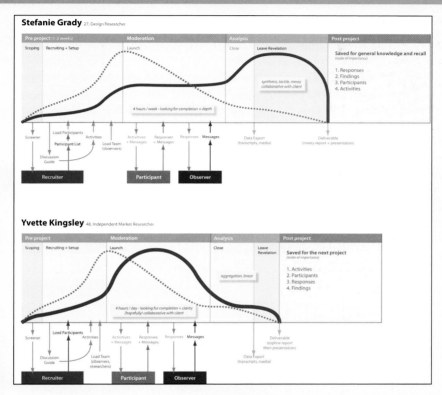

The project had a tight timeline, beginning in June with a release date of September 30th. The development team had successfully implemented an Agile Extreme Programming (XP) process. The design team worked closely with developers, integrating their design work with that methodology. The personas' usage scenarios allowed developers to quickly learn and understand customers' needs and goals. Given the short time frame, decisions needed to be made on which features should be given priority. The team decided that the biggest initial business opportunity resided with market researchers versus design researchers, and so features that spoke to the market researcher persona were prioritized for the initial release. Key path scenarios for the primary persona became Agile's "story cards," allowing the design and development team to collaborate closely and communicate clearly. Features that were more focused toward design researchers were placed lower in the story queue for subsequent development iterations.

Case Study: Revelation PROJECT *(continued)*

The Solution

In four weeks' time, the designers made significant improvements to the product. The Dashboard home page became more action-oriented to better help researchers moderate activities and analyze data. Setting up a research study was streamlined. Researchers are now able to moderate and interact with participants' responses using natural-language statements such as: "Show me what's new" or "Show me all responses tagged with..." or "Show me all responses from this participant...."

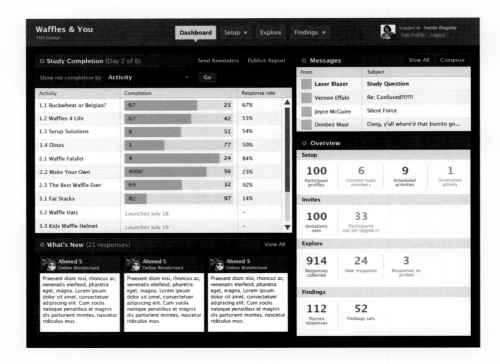

The design team designed multiple analysis tools for researchers and their clients to approach participants' responses from many different angles. PROJECT users can dynamically build data sets around any theme or idea. Research showed that improving collaboration between researchers and their clients was an important opportunity area, and the simpler analysis tools let clients get involved without any training overhead.

Agile

Agile is a particular programming methodology that, as of this writing (2009), is deeply in vogue. It arose in the early 2000s as a reaction to what is known as "Waterfall" methods, wherein developers are handed a large stack of documentation ("functional specifications") and told to build them. (Truthfully, much of the process outlined in this book could be seen as a waterfall-like process.)

The essence of Agile methodology is the breaking of larger tasks/features into small pieces to be built in short bursts of development that typically last from one to four weeks. A small team works on these "iterations" together through the full development cycle: planning, requirements analysis, design, coding, unit testing, and acceptance testing, wherein they demonstrate the working piece to stakeholders. Agile helps minimize overall risk, and more easily allows for changes to the functionality.

What is challenging for designers working in this methodology is that it doesn't allow for the big picture—strategic and frameworks—thinking that designers need to engage in, nor does it seem to provide enough time for ideation and exploring multiple options. An ideal situation is to allow for a more traditional design process (such as outlined in this book) to occur, but then turn to Agile methods (with a designer embedded in the team in order to make changes to the design as necessitated by the code) for development.

Summary

Prototyping, testing, and development are the final crucial steps in the design process, where all the strategy, research, ideation, design principles, and refinement come into their full bloom and the product comes alive. It's important for designers to not abdicate responsibility for the final outcome of their designs to those who build them, for the simple reason that no matter how complete you think your documentation is, developers and manufacturers likely do not have all the information and the product vision you possess.

It's also important to note the "end" of the design process is seldom the end. Products, even after launch, are always evolving and take on a life of their own as users begin to use them in their daily lives. Problems and opportunities will arise, and the market will change. And then the process starts all over again.

For Further Reading

Designing Interfaces, Jenifer Tidwell

Paper Prototyping: The Fast and Easy Way to Design and Refine User Interfaces, Carolyn Snyder

Making Things Talk, Tom Igoe

A Practitioner's Guide to Prototyping, Todd Zaki Warfel

A Practical Guide to Usability Testing, Joseph S. Dumas, Janice C. Redish

The Art of Agile Development, James Shore and Shane Warden

Designing the Moment: Web Interface Design Concepts in Action, Robert Hoekman Jr.

GUI Bloopers 2.0: Common User Interface Design Don'ts and Dos, Jeff Johnson

Don't Make Me Think: A Common Sense Approach to Web Usability, 2nd Edition, Steve Krug

9

The Future of
Interaction Design

The future of interaction design is being created now. Interaction designers on their own or at startup companies or huge organizations are devising products and services that will change how we interact with each other and with our world. It's not hyperbole to suggest that the next 20 years will see significant changes in almost all aspects of our lives: our healthcare experience, how we entertain ourselves, how we shop, how we get from place to place. How, when, and where we receive information will be completely transformed, and interaction designers will be there, to guide and design the products and services that will shape the future.

Interaction designers must take a role not only in creating the future of the discipline, but also in making sure that the future works well and is designed for humans to use and enjoy. The next decades will see some amazing advances, some of which are explored in this chapter. Interaction designers are at the center of all of it. It's an exciting time.

The Internet has moved from behind computer monitors to the objects and buildings that are all around us. Microprocessors, sensors, and networking capabilities such as radio-frequency identification (RFID) tags are being built into everyday objects, creating what many have called the **Internet of Things**. Indeed, we're rapidly moving away from thinking about the Internet less as a destination and more as a utility to be plugged into and used like electricity.

Wireless connections are beginning to blanket our cities (either through monolithic engineering projects or ad-hoc networks patched together by individuals and businesses), allowing for the ability to access information contextually, when and where it is needed, geo-located. We will be able to find people and things, and they will be able to find us.

Our products and services will better adapt to us, and we to them. Robots will perform tasks in our homes, schools, cities, and businesses. Intelligent agents will find information we need before we need it. We will wear our computers on our sleeves, if the computer isn't the sleeve itself.

The future will be what the future has always been: hopeful, scary, unknown, disorienting. Only more so.

The Next Five Years of the Internet

"I live in Walled City," he said.

"Mitsuko told me. That's like a multi-user domain."

"Walled City is unlike anything."

*"Give me the address when I give you the emulator. I'll check it out."
The sidewalk arched over a concrete channel running with grayish
water. It reminded her of her Venice. She wondered if there had
been a stream there once.*

"It has no address," he said.

"That's impossible," Chia said.

He said nothing.

—From *Idoru* by William Gibson

Over the next decade, there will be a wide range of products and services
online, from highly structured to nearly formless. The more "traditional,"
structured products—blogs, home pages, marketing and communication
sites, content sites, search engines, and so on—will have their form and content determined mainly by their designers and creators.

Less structured are rich, desktop-like applications, the more interesting of
which, such as Twitter, are Internet-native and built to take advantage of
the strengths of the Internet: collective actions and data (Amazon's "People
who bought this also bought..."), social communities across wide distances
(Yahoo Groups), aggregation of many sources of data (Google News), near
real-time access to timely data (stock quotes, weather), and easy publishing
of content from one to many (Facebook, Flickr). For many of these products
and services, it is the users who supply the content (such as it is).

And there will also be a new set of products and services, many of which
won't have associated Web sites to visit at all. Instead, there will be loose
collections of application parts, content, and data that don't exist anywhere
really, yet can be located, used, reused, fixed, and remixed. The content people will search for and use may reside on an individual computer, a mobile
phone, or on traffic sensors along a remote highway. Users won't need to
know where these loose bits live; instead, their tools will know.

Tools for the Next Web

These unstructured bits won't be useful without the tools and the knowledge necessary to make sense of them, similar to the way an HTML file doesn't make much sense without a browser to view it. Indeed, many of these bits will be inaccessible or hidden if a user doesn't have the right tools.

This is where interaction designers come in: creating tools for the next generations of the Internet. The tools we'll use to find, read, filter, use, mix, remix, and connect us to the Internet will have to be a lot smarter and do a lot more work than the ones we have now.

Part of that work is in formatting. Who and what determines how something looks and works? With the unstructured bits of content and functionality, perhaps only a veneer of form will remain. How something looks will be an uneasy mix of the data and the tools we use to engage with it. Indeed, visual design is becoming centralized in the tools and methods we use to view and interact with content, moving away from its decentralized locations on Web sites. Already, RSS readers let users customize the way they view feeds from a variety of sources, as do some plug-ins for the Firefox browser. Soon, expect to see this type of customization happening with bits of functionality as well as content.

Web browsers will probably be most affected by these new, varied experiences. Our current browsers were designed for navigating a hypertext content space—structured products and services, in other words. They are poor to merely adequate for Web applications and nearly useless for unstructured products and services. We will need new browsers—new tools altogether—and interaction designers need to be involved in creating them.

It would also be a mistake to think that most of these tools will be on laptop or desktop computers. The number of people online is expected to reach about 2 billion in 2010, and a large percentage of those people will be accessing the Web via mobile phones and devices. The shift away from desktop-like experiences will be profound and require incredible amounts of work from interaction designers to become a reality.

It is more important now than ever before that our digital tools have the characteristics of good interaction design baked into them. These tools will determine what we can do online and how we can do it and what it will feel like. Our online experience will largely be determined by how good these tools are, in much the same way the first 20 years of the Web were shaped by the browsers we used to access it.

Intelligent Agents

Some of these tools will likely be software acting on our behalf. These "intelligent agents" will be a type of application that resides in (and sometimes follows its user between) digital devices. The duty of these agents will be to perform tasks that are impossible or too time-consuming for humans, such as finding, sorting, and filtering every blog post about interaction design ever posted, or constantly monitoring networks for problems. These agents will monitor our behavior and gather and use information for us before we need it. They will watch over our devices, our homes, and even our physical health.

What's being called the **Semantic Web** will help fulfill this prediction. Currently, Web pages are mostly designed to be read by people, not machines. The Semantic Web would change this, so that software including intelligent agents can use the Internet more effectively. The Semantic Web consists of online content understandable by computers, so that they can perform more of the tedious work involved in finding, sharing, and combining information. Using the Semantic Web, for example, an agent could find the restaurant closest to your current location and make a reservation based on your schedule.

Of course, having semi-autonomous agents roaming online doing things that the user may be only dimly aware of is a frightening prospect. Users will want to make sure that these agents aren't doing wrong things on their behalf. The interaction designers who will be involved in creating these agents will also have to design the means for users to supervise and control their agents. This is a design challenge still waiting to be fully explored.

Spimes and the Internet of Things

Novelist-cum-design-critic Bruce Sterling has said in his book *Shaping Things* (and elsewhere) that interaction designers will be creating and working with a type of object that he calls a **spime**. Spimes are networked, context-aware, self-monitoring, self-documenting, uniquely identified objects that exude data about themselves and their environments. Spimes reveal every piece of metadata (their location, their owner, the date they were made, usage patterns, and so on) about themselves. They can be tracked through space (the "sp-" part of the term) and time (the "-ime" part) throughout their entire lifecycles, from their prototypes to their eventual destruction.

These spimes will likely have self-identifiers and networking capabilities that allow them to communicate. Using sensors and wireless technology, they will communicate with each other and the Internet like a swarm. Spimes, and other objects similarly enabled, will be able to be located and have information added to them, such as "These are my shoes."

Spimes will create an informational Web—the Internet of Things—the uses (and abuses) for which boggle the mind. Imagine having a list of every item in your house, down to the smallest pack of matches. Lose your mobile phone in a taxi? Simply find where it is in real time.

> NOTE *Of course, the privacy issues related to an Internet of Things boggle the mind as well. Imagine thieves being able to find all the most expensive items within several blocks, or governments being able easily and instantly to know everything about you, down to what you have in your refrigerator.*

The data that this Internet of Things will reveal will be fascinating and frightening. Sterling uses the example of tennis shoes. Spime tennis shoes, over time, could reveal what happens to their rubber soles at the end of their life cycle: are they being recycled into playground coverings or are they becoming aerosol carcinogens? Using this data, we will be able to see with clarity the impact of products on our world. Spimes offer the possibility of accountability in products.

As designers such as Adam Greenfield (see the interview later in this chapter) have noted, what is missing from the idea of an Internet of Things (or at least from the nomenclature) is *people*. How do people work with, understand, and affect an Internet of Things? While things may have meaning in and of themselves, they derive an additional layer of meaning when used by people. How interaction designers place human beings into the Internet of Things is a challenge for the future.

Human-Robot Interactions

Robots are no longer the science-fiction machines of yore, nor are they used only to create cars in factories. Robots—broadly defined as programmable machines that can perform specific physical tasks—are among us, likely for good. A robot, however, is more than just an object. It is both a product and a service.

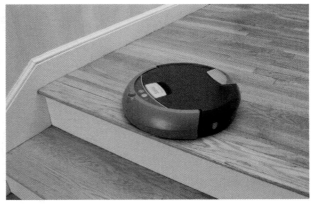

Robots are being designed and built all over the globe: as floor cleaners (**Figure 9.1**), toys (**Figure 9.2**), musical instruments (**Figure 9.3**), and more. Because of the complex issues surrounding robots, from the emotional to the technical, interaction designers need to become more involved in their creation and use.

Figure 9.1

iRobot's Scooba is a floor-washing robot that can prep, wash, scrub, and dry hard floors, all at the touch of a button.

Figure 9.2

Lego Mindstorms allow children and hobbyists to create sophisticated robots easily.

Figure 9.3

ForestBot is a robotic installation by the music/technology group League of Electronic Musical Urban Robots (LEMUR). ForestBot is a collection of 25 ten-foot stalks that each have an egg-shaped rattle mounted on the free end.

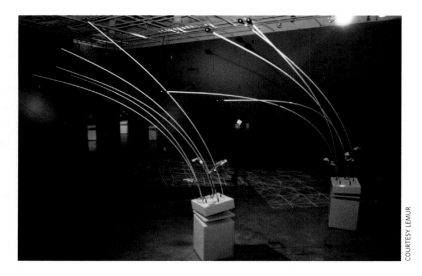

COURTESY LEMUR

Figure 9.4

Carnegie Mellon's roboreceptionist gives directions, answers the phone, and even gossips about her "life."

Interaction designers need to be aware of two factors when designing robots: autonomy and social interaction. Autonomy gives the robot the ability to act on the user's behalf without direct external control. Robots like those from Lego Mindstorms have very little autonomy, but some "robots," such as pacemakers and artificial hearts, have full autonomy—their human users don't have to tell them to work. Similarly, there are robots, like the toy Furby, that engage in little reciprocal interaction, and others, like Carnegie Mellon's Valerie, the robot receptionist (**Figure 9.4**), designed specifically to interact with humans.

Robot designer and professor Jodi Forlizzi has outlined three main design issues with robots[1]:

▶   **Form.** Does the robot have a humanlike appearance? How big is it? What are its physical characteristics, such as size, shape, scale, and material?

▶   **Function.** How does the robot communicate and express itself? Does it use sound, motion, gesture, light, color, or scent?

▶   **Manner of behavior.** How does the robot behave and in what situations? How does it go about its activities and how does it interact with humans? How social is it?

---

1   See her design work with robots at http://goodgestreet.com/research/ppr.html

Carl DiSalvo on Designing for Robots

Carl DiSalvo is an assistant professor at Georgia Tech University whose work focuses on the existing and potential uses of emerging technologies such as robotics, sensing, visualization, and mapping in the urban environment. Previously, Carl worked as a designer for MetaDesign and as a consultant for the Walker Art Center's New Media Initiatives. In 2006, he received a Ph.D. in Design from Carnegie Mellon University. As a graduate student, he worked as a design research associate on the Project on People and Robots at the CMU Human-Computer Interaction Institute.

Briefly describe the realm of robots. What type of robots are being made or planned?

We can make some distinctions among robots, but none of them are mutually exclusive. A robot could, and often does, fall into two or more of categories. For example, there are social robots, service robots, and field robots. Many of these distinctions actually relate to the research question at hand more than to a kind of consumer product. This of course reflects the fact that outside of a few domains and a few choice examples, robots still are primarily research endeavors.

The most common domains for contemporary robotic products are military or industrial settings. Robots are also beginning to be used in medicine and scientific exploration. And of course toys. Robots for the home consumer, such as the Roomba, are still uncommon. For example, there are a handful of vacuum and lawn-mowing robots, but other than that, except for toys, there aren't really robots, as we commonly think of them, in the home.

What type of design work is being done with robots now?

All kinds. This is what makes robotics so exciting. The challenges and opportunities of robotics sweep across every field of design. Perhaps the most obvious is the work in industrial design in creating the visual form of the robot. The industrial design of a robot is an example of styling visual form with significant impact on interaction. In fact, it's difficult to separate industrial design from interaction design in robots. Because of the newness of robotics and the public's unfamiliarity with robots, the visual form of the robot often takes precedence in shaping our expectations of the robot and how we interact with the product.

In addition to designing the visual form of the robot, there is a lot of interface design involved with robots: interfaces for tele-operation as well as interfaces for direct interaction. These interfaces might be screen-based, physical, voice, or some combination of the three. Because we have yet to arrive at any standards for, or even common experiences of, interacting with a robot interface, interaction design for robotics is open to broad inquiry and invention.

How is designing for robots different from designing other products?

Robots are hyperboles of the products contemporary designers are challenged with. That is, they are an exaggeration of the contemporary products because robots are "everything all at once": complex embodied technological artifacts that require significant design knowledge of industrial, communication, interaction, and service design, potent cultural icons, and, too, the most mundane of gadgets.

All of the diverse elements of a product are brought together and amplified in a robot. This presents a nearly unique challenge and opportunity. Designing robots requires a level of synthesis not often encountered in other products.

What will be the role of interaction designers in this field in the future?

In many ways, robots are still fictional entities, at least when it comes to common consumer products. Interaction designers have the opportunity to invent what these new products of the future might or should be like. This comes along with significant responsibility to shape these products in ways that are not merely seductive but appropriate.

One of the most pressing needs concerning the design of robots, concerning design in general, is to consider how these nascent technologies become products, and in the process to take up the opportunity to critically engage these technologies, rather than simply striving forward with unreflective novelty.

Wearables

Your next computer might be a size 10.

Although the idea of wearable computing has been around since the early 1960s, it wasn't until 2005, when Adidas introduced Adidas_1 (**Figure 9.5**), a running shoe with a microprocessor that adjusts the cushioning of the shoe based on its use, that the idea of wearables reached the public consciousness. Likely, Adidas succeeded because the Adidas_1 looks stylish, unlike many previous attempts at wearables: clunky pieces of gear awkwardly strapped to some geek's body.

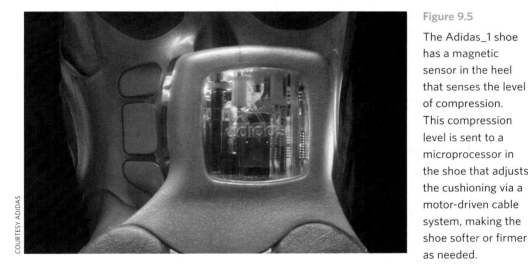

COURTESY ADIDAS

Figure 9.5

The Adidas_1 shoe has a magnetic sensor in the heel that senses the level of compression. This compression level is sent to a microprocessor in the shoe that adjusts the cushioning via a motor-driven cable system, making the shoe softer or firmer as needed.

Designers of wearables take as their starting point the fact that the thing most people have with them most of the time is their clothes. Why not, then, use clothing as a platform for technology so that we have things that we need with us all the time? Computers in clothing can adjust the clothing to project messages, react to other devices, or change according to the weather or the wearer's mood (**Figure 9.6**).

Figure 9.6

F+R Hugs ("The Hug Shirt") is a shirt that allows people to send and receive the physical sensation of a hug over long distances. Embedded in the shirt are sensors that feel the hug's strength, the skin's warmth, and the heartbeat rate of the sender. Actuators re-create those sensations in the shirt of the distant loved one.

COURTESY CUTECIRCUIT

Of course, wearables don't have to be clothing per se. BodyMedia's GoWear products (**Figure 9.7**) are small devices that strap on an arm and monitor the wearer's health. Wristwatches have been a basis for wearables, such as Fossil's WristPDA.

Figure 9.7

The GoWear® fit Armband uses a multisensor array to collect continuous physiological data directly from the wearer's skin. Users can monitor their energy expenditure (calories burned), duration of physical activity, number of steps taken, sleep/wake states, and more.

COURTESY BODYMEDIA

The challenges for interaction designers working with wearables are many, as are the opportunities. Designers have to pay particular attention not only to functionality, but also to form. Wearables, unlike devices that sit on a desk or slip into a pocket or purse, are meant to be, well, *worn*. And things worn on the body for long periods of time need to be durable, stylish, and unobtrusive. Their context is anywhere that humans are, and that is an extremely broad and varied set of environments. The opportunity with wearables is that people don't need to be concerned about "another device to carry." Users won't have to carry anything except the clothes they wear or something strapped to their bodies like a fashion accessory. Information and functionality move with the user, available when needed, and data is captured from the user's body and location that might never be captured otherwise.

Wearables also allow interaction designers to take advantage of more parts of the body than they are used to engaging. A glove with sensors might unlock doors with a flick of a finger. A sleeve might become a screen for projecting images, and a necklace, like Microsoft Research's SenseCam,[2] might take thousands of pictures a day, allowing users to replay their days visually if they choose.

Ubiquitous Computing

Over the past 60 years, the ratio of humans to computers has radically changed. In the early years of computing, the ratio of humans to computers was many to one: many people worked on one mainframe computer. Then came the era of the personal computer, and the ratio changed to one to one: people who used computers had their own on their desks. Recently, however, and in the future this will be even more true, the ratio has changed so that one person now has many "computers" under his or her control: a laptop, digital camera, MP3 player, mobile phone, car, microwave, television, and on and on. In the words of Mark Weiser, the Xerox PARC scientist who wrote the seminal papers[3] on the subject, most of these computers are "invisible, yet all around us."

The era of ubiquitous computing (or **ubicomp**) has, like so much of the "future" technology in this chapter, already started; it just isn't widespread yet. As microprocessors and sensors grow ever cheaper and also more powerful, it isn't a stretch to imagine the ratio of humans to computers becoming one to thousands. Most of these "computers" will be embedded in the products we own, and aside from the behavior they afford, they will be imperceptible to us. We won't be controlling them via a keyboard and mouse either. As described in Chapter 7, these interfaces will often have no faces; we'll engage with them using voice, touch, and gestures.

---

2 http://research.microsoft.com/en-us/um/cambridge/projects/sensecam/
3 Such as "The Computer for the 21st Century" in *Scientific American* Special Issue on Communications, Computers, and Networks, September 1991

Interaction designers have a major part to play in the design of ubicomp systems, and it is an exciting and interesting time. While you get ready in the morning, your bathroom mirror might show you your calendar, the weather report for the day, and perhaps e-mail from your friends. The bus stop might indicate when the next bus will arrive and how crowded it is. The bus itself might have digital notes on it left by passengers ("This seat is broken"). At your office, a wall might be your monitor, turning on simply when you tell it to. Meeting rooms might automatically record what is said and drawn on digital whiteboards. Any room you are in throughout the day might play music of your choice and adjust to the temperature you like based on the clothes you are wearing.

This scenario sounds to us now like science fiction or those AT&T "You Will" commercials from the early 1990s,[4] but it likely isn't too far off, and each of these moments will need the skills and talents of interaction designers to make them easy to use, fun, and appropriate. How do you change the bathroom mirror from displaying the weather report to displaying e-mail? How do riders leave or see messages left on a bus? The incredible range of design opportunities is apparent.

Frankly, the stakes are simply too high in ubicomp for interaction designers not to be involved. In a typical interaction with a digital device right now, users are in control of the engagement. They determine when the engagement stops and starts. They control how the computer (and through the computer, others) sees and experiences them. Users' bodies, except for their hands and eyes, are for the most part irrelevant. None of this is true in ubicomp.

Users may step into a room and unknowingly begin to engage with a ubicomp system—or many systems. The thermostat, door, light fixture, television, and so on may all be part of different systems, wired to respond to a person's presence. Where users are in the room—even the direction they are facing—may matter. Standing near the television and facing it may trigger it to turn on, as could a particular gesture, such as pretending to click a remote control in the air. But because users may not know any of this, they have no way of controlling how they present themselves to the system. Perhaps they don't want the room to know they are there!

---

4 Watch them online at www.youtube.com/watch?v=TZb0avfQme8

The implications of ubicomp are profound, and it will be up to interaction designers to make these systems discoverable, recoverable, safe, and humane. Like robots, ubicomp systems are often both products and services, so all the skills, methods, and techniques discussed throughout this book (and more) will be needed to design them in a way that works for humans. One can easily imagine how ubicomp systems could get out of control, embarrassing and annoying us. Our privacy will be impinged upon every day, and ubicomp is hard to see without signage systems and icons on objects and in areas to let us know we are in an ubicomp environment. We will need to know what is being observed, and how, and where, but without filling our rooms with signs.

Interaction designers need to design ways for people not only to understand these systems, but also to gain access to them if problems occur. When problems happen—the system keeps switching off the TV every time you sneeze!—how can they be corrected? Is it the lamp that controls the TV or is it the wall?

Another challenge in designing for ubicomp is that most ubicomp systems will likely be **stateless**, meaning that they will be much more moment-to-moment than current systems are. Users won't be able to refer to an earlier moment and revert to that, or at least not easily, making it harder to undo mistakes—"Wait, what did I just say that caused all the windows of the room to open?" or "Pretend I didn't just walk into this room." Interaction designers will need to take this feature of ubicomp systems into account and design without the benefits of Undo commands and Back buttons.

It is incumbent upon interaction designers to instill meaning and values into ubicomp more than any other system. When the things around us are aware, monitoring us and capable of turning our offices, homes, and public spaces into nightmares of reduced civil liberties and insane levels of personalization ("Hi Sarah! Welcome back to the bus! I see you are wearing jeans today. Mind if I show you some ads for Levi's?"), interaction designers need to have compassionate respect for the people who will be engaged with them, some of them unwillingly and unknowingly.

Adam Greenfield on Everyware

Adam Greenfield is an internationally recognized writer, user experience consultant, and critical futurist. Before his current position as head of design direction for service and user-interface design at Nokia, he was lead information architect for the Tokyo office of Web consultancy Razorfish; prior to that, he worked as senior information architect for marchFIRST, also in Tokyo. He's also been, at various points in his career, a rock critic for SPIN *magazine, a medic at the Berkeley Free Clinic, a coffeehouse owner in West Philadelphia, and a PSYOP sergeant in the U.S. Army's Special Operations Command.*

What do interaction designers need to know about ubiquitous computing, what you call "everyware?"

Probably the single most important thing that we need to wrap our heads around is *multiplicity*.

Instead of the neatly circumscribed space of interaction between a single user and his or her PC, his or her mobile device, we're going to have to contend with a situation in which multiple users are potentially interacting with multiple technical systems in a given space at a given moment.

This has technical implications, of course, in terms of managing computational resources and so on, but for me the most interesting implications concern the quality of user experience. How can we best design informational systems so that they (a) work smoothly in synchrony with *each other*, and (b) deliver optimal experiences to the overburdened human at their focus? This is the challenge that Mark Weiser and John Seely Brown refer to as "encalming, as well as informing," and I think it's one we've only begun to scratch the surface of addressing.

How will the interactions we have with digital products now differ from those in the future?

The simple fact that networked information-processing devices are going to be deployed everywhere in the built environment rather strongly implies the inadequacy of the traditional user interface modalities we've been able to call on, most particularly keyboards and keypads.

Adam Greenfield on Everyware *(continued)*

When a room, or a lamppost, or a running shoe is, in and of itself, an information gathering, processing, storage, and transmission device, it's crazy to assume that the keyboard or the traditional GUI makes sense as a channel for interaction—somewhat akin to continuing to think of a car as a "horseless carriage." We're going to need to devise ways to interact with artifacts like these that are sensitive to the way we use them, biomechanically, psychologically, and socially. Especially if we want the systems we design to encalm their users, we're going to need to look somewhere else.

Voice and gestural interfaces, in this context, are very appealing candidates, because they so easily accommodate themselves to a wide variety of spaces and contexts, without taking up physical space, or preventing the user from attending to more focal tasks. They become particularly interesting given the expansion in the number of child, elderly, or nonliterate users implied by the increased ambit of post-PC informatics.

You've spoken about "design dissolving into behavior." How can interaction designers accomplish that?

Well, that's a notion of Naoto Fukasawa's, that interactions with designed systems can be so well thought out by their authors, and so effortless on the part of their users, that they effectively abscond from awareness.

Following him, I define everyware at its most refined as "information processing dissolving in behavior." We see this, for example, in Hong Kong, where women leave their RFID-based Octopus cards in their handbags and simply swing their bags across the readers as they move through the turnstiles. There's a very sophisticated transaction between card and reader there, but it takes 0.2 seconds, and it's been subsumed entirely into this very casual, natural, even jaunty gesture.

But that wasn't designed. It just emerged; people figured how to do that by themselves, without some designer having to instruct them in the nuances. So I'd argue that creating experiences with ubiquitous systems that are of similar quality and elegance is largely a matter of close and careful attention to the way people already use the world. The more we can accommodate and not impose, the more successful our designs will be.

Summary

"The best way to predict the future," said Alan Kay, the Xerox PARC scientist who came up with the idea of a laptop computer, the Dynabook, in 1972, "is to invent it." The future arrives, second by second, whether we want it to or not, and it is the job of interaction designers to invent it, or at least to make it more humane. The sheer number of products and services, augmented by new technologies, that will become widely available in the next decade and their likely effect on the world will be staggering. Between the advancing technology and the people who will use it stand interaction designers, shaping, guiding, cajoling the future into forms for humans.

But forget the future—the present is complicated and sophisticated enough. The skills required to use the technology that is available now are far beyond those of most people. Not only are our devices too difficult to use, it is too challenging to tap into the available technology to do something personal. We need tools for making tools.

Interaction designers need to find ways to make the already amazing technology we have available *right now* to the billions of people who don't yet have a way to make this technology their own, to create things that, because of their personal nature, have little or no commercial value but great human value. Interaction designers need to make sure that the already wide so-called digital divide between those who have and can use technology and those who thus far cannot gets no wider. Those people—and we are surrounded by them every day—need the tools to make technology relevant to them and their lives.

For Further Reading

Everyware, Adam Greenfield

Shaping Things, Bruce Sterling

How To Survive a Robot Uprising: Tips on Defending Yourself Against the Coming Rebellion, Daniel H. Wilson

The Big Switch: Rewiring the World, from Edison to Google, Nicholas Carr

Tomorrow Now: Envisioning the Next 50 Years, Bruce Sterling

Wired for War: The Robotics Revolution and Conflict in the 21st Century, P. W. Singer

Epilogue

Designing for Good

What responsibility do interaction designers have for what they design? Some designers think that the products and services they create are morally neutral, that users themselves and society, not the designer, should determine how a product should be used. But what if the user's task is to injure someone? Or if the system being designed helps people do harm?

The book *IBM and the Holocaust* by Edwin Black relates the story of a timber merchant from Bendzin, Poland, who, in August 1943, arrived at the Nazi concentration camp at Auschwitz as a prisoner. There, the Nazis assigned him a five-digit IBM Hollerith number, 44673. This number was later tattooed on his forearm. This number, and the thousands like it, were part of a custom punch card system specifically designed by IBM to track prisoners in Nazi concentration camps. (In the IBM system, the Auschwitz camp code was 001.) The Hollerith system tracked prisoners and their availability for work, their punch card numbers following them from labor assignment to labor assignment until most of them were put to death.

The Holocaust was extremely well-designed.

When we think of good design, we usually mean products and services that help users complete their tasks in an efficient, effective, aesthetically-pleasing manner. But there is another definition of "good" that should be considered when designing: the moral, the just, the life-affirming. The good that protects human dignity.

Interaction designers should design for this sort of good as well.

Ethics in Design

Any serious examination of interaction design has to include a discussion about ethics. Ethics are how designers can distinguish between good and bad design. It's about how designers should respond when asked to do work that is questionable. In short, it's about consequences; if there were no consequences to interaction design, there'd be no need for ethics. And with the dawning of the age of ubiquitous computing, mobile devices that can track our movements, and robots, wearables, and intelligent agents that have access to our homes and our most private secrets, the consequences for interaction design are becoming more far-reaching and more significant than they have ever been.

Ethics is about human decision making: why and how we make the decisions we do. It is about determining what is the *right* thing to do in given circumstances. Design theorist Richard Buchanan has noted[1] that this is the same activity interaction designers do all the time: determine the right thing to do considering the given constraints. To design is to make ethical choices. In other words, design *is* ethics.

Principles

To be an interaction designer requires principles, because interaction designers guide what the interactions between people *should* be via the products and services they create. Are some people more deserving of respect than others? Is it OK to make the product good for some people, but less so for others? These are the types of issues that, knowingly or (usually) unknowingly, interaction designers deal with all the time, and it requires principles on the part of the designer to sort them out.

Principles for interaction designers are made up of a complex set of guides, including the personal beliefs of the designer, codes of ethics from professional organizations like the Industrial Designers Society of America (IDSA), and governmental and societal standards for safety and usability. Without a firm set of their own principles, interaction designers can find themselves adopting the beliefs and values of the companies they work for, and this can be a dangerous course, as shown above with the IBM-designed system for the Nazis. There needs to be a balance between the ethics of designers and the ethics of the organizations that employ them.

Deliberate Choices

Interaction designers try to promote certain kinds of interactions between people. Thus, the fundamental ethical guide for interaction designers should be *the quality of those interactions*, on both sides of the equation—the person initiating the interaction (such as the e-mail sender) and the person receiving the action (such as the e-mail receiver). The content of the communication aside (e-mail spam, say), the quality of those interactions is strongly determined by the decisions the designer makes while designing the product or service. Thought of this way, even the placement of

---

1   See his essays "Human Dignity and Human Rights: Thoughts on the Principles of Human-Centered Design" and "Design Ethics"

buttons on an interface is an ethical act. Does the designer have respect and compassion for the users? Does this product or service give the users their human dignity? In short, is the design *good*? Good for the users, good for those indirectly affected, good for the culture, good for the environment?

The choices interaction designers make need to be deliberate and forward-thinking. Random choices ("Because I like it" or "It's always been done this way") are the death of design and an abdication of responsibility. Designers need to consider the consequences of their design decisions. Designers have a **sacred trust** with the users of their products and services. Every time users perform an action with a designed product or service, they are, indirectly, trusting the designer who created it to have done her job, and done it ethically. Users trust that not only will the task they want to do be accomplished (an e-mail will get sent and arrive at its destination), but they also trust that those products and services (and by extension the designers who designed them) will do them no harm. Users entrust designers (through the products and services they design) with intensely personal information—passwords, bank account numbers, credit card numbers, and so on—and, in some cases, with their lives. Designers need to recognize and respect that trust.

It isn't enough, however, to only do right by the individual users. Individual users (and the organizations that may be behind them) may not have the best interests of others at heart. Although people will always find ways to use products and services in ways that they weren't designed for, designers need to be cognizant of the negative consequences their designs may cause to those who aren't users or who are forced users—like the timber merchant from Bendzin, Poland, Hollerith number 44673.

But just as there are forces for evil in this world, so are there forces for good. After the carnage and atrocities of World War II, representatives from 50 countries met in April 1945, only a few miles from where I'm writing this in San Francisco, to design a service to humanity, something that would help prevent anything like what had happened twice in the 20th century from ever happening again. Something that would facilitate and inspire dialog—interactions—between countries. Their work, their design, became the United Nations. And while the United Nations—like all things made by humans—is flawed and imperfect, its goals of and actions towards international cooperation, peaceful conflict resolution, human rights, and humanitarian aid are a force for good in the world. May the products that interaction designers create all be thus.

Index